The Weaponization of AI and the Internet

How Global Networks of Infotech Overlords Are Expanding Their Control Over Our Lives

Larry Bell

The Weaponization of AI and the Internet: How Global Networks of Infotech Overlords Are Expanding Their Control Over Our Lives

Other books by Larry Bell:

Reinventing Ourselves: How Technology is Rapidly and Radically Transforming Humanity
Scared Witless: Prophets and Profits of Climate Doom
Climate of Corruption: Politics and Power behind the Global Warming Hoax
Cosmic Musings: Contemplating Life beyond Self
Reflections on Oceans and Puddles: One Hundred Reasons to be Enthusiastic, Grateful and Hopeful
Thinking Whole: Rejecting Half-Witted Left & Right Brain Limitations

STAIRWAY PRESS—Apache Junction

Book Cover Art: Albert Rajkumar
Cover Design by Chris Benson
www.BensonCreative.com

STAIRWAY≡PRESS
www.StairwayPress.com
1000 West Apache Trail, Suite 126
Apache Junction, AZ 85120

Dedication

To all of us who must sort out and adapt to blindingly rapid technological advancements with consequences that forever transform unfathomably broad aspects of human society and values—for better and worse.

Key among these are inevitable trend-vector tradeoffs between traditional expectations of personal privacy versus our desires for convenience and privacy.

It's a Devil's bargain.

Introduction

HUMANITY IS EXPERIENCING the very earliest beginnings of an expansively transformative and disruptive information revolution. Machine learning is accelerating artificial intelligence (AI) applications at an exponential clip.

Remote surveillance and monitoring technologies—combined with incomprehensibly massive data storage capacities—follow and record us virtually everywhere, even in our homes. Algorithms that respond to our information requests also listen in on our private conversations and snitch on us to uninvited outsiders.

Electronic eavesdroppers catalog our special interests and even analyze our psychological profiles in order to micro-target us for product and political commercials. Automated monitors programmed to identify disagreement with certain political views can censure our private social media exchanges.

AI "bots" can now mimic individual human voices. Political regimes can apply such fakery to produce video as well as audio impersonations of opposition targets for propaganda purposes.

The global emergence of "smart cities" now connect together and integrate all these capabilities within seamless Internet-of-Things (IoT) networks. Such developments openly invite autocratic regimes to weave these diverse data streams into web grids of social control.

Those who develop and administer these capabilities are exerting growing influence over broad aspects of our lives. In the process, a tiny group is amassing unimaginably huge global economic and political power. These infotech overlords and their cohorts wield enormous financial and technical resources to help tip elections in ways they favor. They also control intrusive cyber networks to dig up dirt on candidates they don't like.

As warned by the international nonprofit Internet of Things Forum, the qualitative shift in people's lives brought about by smart devices, offices and cities will bring about the extreme diminishment of private spaces, which warrants urgent attention.[i]

In my recent book *Reinventing Ourselves: How Technology is Rapidly and Radically Transforming Humanity*, I refer to the big tradeoff between more technological convenience for less privacy as a "boiling frog" analogy.

Like that hapless critter in a shallow pan of water placed over a flame, we complacently adjust to the gradual temperature change until it's too late to jump out.

Christof Koch, chief scientist and president of the Allen Institute of Brain Science in Seattle, observes that sweeping societal and economic influences of AI and the Internet signal a fourth industrial revolution. The first, powered by the steam engine, moved us from agriculture to urban societies. The second, powered by electricity, ushered in mass production and created a consumer culture. The third, centered on computers and the Internet, shifted the economy from manufacturing to services.[ii]

Many people appropriately worry that this most recent revolution will have innumerable and far-reaching disruptive effects on society—putting people out of work, adding to income inequality and some will say, even posing an existential risk to the ultimate future of Homo sapiens.

Others remind us that just as all previous technical revolutions profoundly increased human productivity, wellbeing and lifespans, this one will as well. For example, just as the third revolution eliminated some jobs, it also created opportunities for new ones. Once again, AI will produce demands for even more rewarding work, and in the process, will make life better for almost everyone.

Exercised through the minds, hands and free choices of the many, such benefits are limitless. Controlled by the special interests and agendas of but a few, their applications for social control and exploitation are equally boundless.

Whereas this book emphasizes many serious downsides, risks

and consequences, it is not intended to impugn the morality nor beneficial motivations of the vast majority of organizations and individuals who develop, implement and coordinate these marvelous new information tools and services.

Sadly, wonderful innovations of progress for many also become weapons of abuse when applied irresponsibly by a tiny few. Automobiles operated by drunkards and other fools recklessly endanger all motorists. Firearms purchased by law-abiding hunters, self-defense owners and recreational shooters become weapons of aggression in the hands of those who are intent on harming defenseless targets. Social media, which connects all of us together, becomes divisive and brutal when used for cyberbullying and malicious slander.

Nefarious government regimes are already weaponizing these remarkable technologies and networks to impose intrusive surveillance and oppressive control over their captive citizenry. Concurrently, more and more people everywhere are becoming disposed to trade away precious personal freedoms, including privacy, for promises of increased convenience, efficiency, safety and security from criminal predators.

This book endeavors to recognize the good, bad and conditional aspects of various infotech advances and applications along with their agents of influence over all of our lives.

We have already witnessed a worldwide impact of artificial intelligence over just the last few years to the point that it dominates nearly all businesses, investments and even ethical narratives. As a result, two opposing attitudes appear to have emerged: one believing that AI will beneficially augment humans; the other that it will diminish them.

Both forecasts are likely to prove correct.

As with all revolutions, there again will be winners and losers, beneficiaries and casualties, rewards and costs. Inevitably, our children and theirs' will live with the outcomes of early foundations and safeguards our precedents will forever establish.

[i] *Clearly Opaque: Privacy Risks of the IoT*, the Internet of Things Forum, 2018, https://www.iotprivacyforum.org/clearlyopaque/

[ii] https://alleninstitute.org/what-we-do/brain-science/about/team/staff-profiles/christof-koch/

Table of Contents

THE RACE TO OUTSMART OURSELVES

WILL THE RAPID computing evolutions ultimately revolt against us as HAL did against the Discovery One astronaut crew in the movie "2001: A Space Odyssey," based upon Arthur C. Clarke's novel series?

As you may recall, HAL 9000 (the Heuristically programmed Algorithmic computer) decided to kill the astronauts by locking them outside the spacecraft during a repair after reading their lips to discover a secret plan to disconnect the robotic system's cognitive circuits following lack of trust triggered by a computing glitch. HAL also attempts to suffocate hibernating onboard crewmembers by disconnecting their life support systems.

Fortunately, in this case, human dexterity wins the day. One of the astronauts circumvents HAL's control by manually opening an emergency airlock, detaching a door via its explosive bolts, reentering Discovery and quickly re-pressurizing the airlock.

Whew!

Nevertheless, can we truly blame HAL for its lack of empathy or gratitude for its mentally inferior human creators? If they were smarter, wouldn't HAL's programmers recognize the risk that artificial intelligence might inevitably surpass the capabilities of our human "general intelligence"?

I don't mean to impugn the high quality of general intelligence attributed to HAL's inventors at the University of Illinois, my own alma mater and where I scored a couple of degrees followed by a nearly decade-long stint as a professor. And I'm sure that they wouldn't have intentionally programmed in a resentful sense of robotic alienation towards HAL's intellectually inferior human spacefaring bosses.

But what about the more modern versions of HALs and HILLORYs now referred to as our "voice assistants" which go by such names as Siri, Alexa and Cortana? Can we really trust them?

After all, their human-mimicking voices sound very friendly—and they obviously know a lot of stuff, including the best travel routes to almost everywhere as they patiently correct our dumb driving mistakes.

Meanwhile, they also track our movements and can listen in wherever we are. Many can already anticipate what we may wish to discuss based upon past information requests. Very soon, their interactive conversations with us will become indistinguishable from chats with caring friends.

Do be advised, however, that we may be wise not to trust them to hold those friendly conversations confidential. In addition to being developed to retrieve information, arrange appointments, provide driving directions, play our favorite music, and remind us of scheduled appointments, they also can and do whisper our personal matters to others behind our backs.

So maybe be a little careful when engaged in private telephone conversations. That "person" you think you are sharing secrets with might actually be an AI-minded algorithm-programmed robotic replica of your imagined friend with unfriendly intentions.

So, who do these artificial versions of what we regard to be "real" intelligence finally report to?

Much more about this (and them) later.

First, let's briefly consider what characteristics constitute real versus artificial versions that we believe makes us special. For instance, will computers always depend upon us to teach them?

Actually, many already teach themselves, and in the process, learn much faster than we do.

Moreover, within but a few past decades our machines were beginning to outthink some top human experts in certain very complicated mental challenges:

By 1997, a "Deep Blue" IBM computer defeated the reigning world chess champion, Garry Kasparov.

In 2011, "Watson," another IBM computer, beat all humans in the quiz show Jeopardy.

In 2016, an "AlphaGo" algorithm developed by "DeepMind," a London AI company, dispatched Lee Sedol, a top player in the ancient and complex board game "Go." The algorithm was originally trained on 160,000 games from a database of previously-played games.

The program was later upgraded to "AlphaGo Zero," which taught itself by playing four million games against itself entirely by trial and error. AlphaGo Zero subsequently annihilated its parent, AlphaGo, 100 games to zero. What it learned in less than one month would have required a decade or two of training for a human.

In 2017, "Libratus" software developed at Carnegie Mellon University beat four top players over a 20-day tournament of No-Limit Texas Hold'em poker. The code doesn't need to bluff...it just out-thinks humans.[1]

There is virtually no likelihood that the AI revolutionary march of encroachment upon the human domain of activities will lose momentum. As Professor Justin Zobel, head of the Department of Computing & Information Systems at the University of Melbourne, Australia observes:

It is a truism that computing continues to change our

> *world. It shapes how objects are designed, what information we receive, how and where we work, and who we meet and do business with. And computing changes our understanding of the world around us and the Universe beyond.*[2]

Writing in the *Wall Street Journal*, Committee for Justice President Curt Levy and the Niskanen Center's Ryan Hagemann posit a challenge to ensure that future AI algorithms with minds of their own remain accountable to transparent oversight.

The authors' greatest concern isn't that these advanced computers we create will go rogue and turn against us like HAL did. They instead foresee a greater threat: that AI complexity enables developers to secretly "rig" a system to the advantage of special interests, like manipulating its operating programs to reveal inside information to outside snoops.[3]

Thinking Machines? Really?

A group of scientists, mathematicians and engineers from many organizations held the first meeting of a series at Dartmouth College in 1956 to consider a rather preposterous idea. They wondered if it might be possible to create "thinking machines" that could duplicate or surpass human intellectual capacities.

Two years later, Jack St. Clair Kilby, an electrical engineer at Texas Instruments, came up with another radical idea. He stayed in the lab during a company vacation break and cobbled together a calculating device that combined a transistor, a capacitor and three resistors on a single piece of germanium—the first integrated circuit. It wasn't particularly small—about a half-inch long, but narrow—and not very elegant either. With wires sticking out, it resembled an upside-down cockroach glued to a glass slide.

In January 1959, Bob Noyce at Fairchild Semiconductor in Palo Alto, California developed a precision photographic printing technique using glass as insulation to deposit tiny aluminum wires above silicon transistors without the messy cockroach legs. Kilby's integrated circuit was transformed into a rapidly producible integrated chip with wires 20 times smaller.

The following year, Texas Instruments introduced a Type 502 Flip Flop with one bit of memory that sold for $450. Weeks later, Fairchild produced its own model which was used by other computer companies, the U.S. Air Force and NASA's Apollo rockets.

One bit soon grew to four, then to 16, then to 64. This capacity increase occurred as the chips continued to rapidly shrink in size. According to a 1965 prediction by Fairchild research director Gordon Moore, now referred to as "Moore's Law," the chips' information density would double every 18 to 24 months. By 1969, the TI 3101 64-bit memory chip was priced at $1 a bit. Your iPhone probably has a trillion bits priced at merely pico cents each.

A new so-called "digital computer revolution" first emerged in the commonplace public lexicon to describe rapid micro-processing-based advancements which began to occur during the 1970s and 1980s. Prior to that time, the only contact most people had with computers was through utility bills, banks and payroll services or computer-generated junk mail.

Modern microcomputer ancestors used early integrated circuit (microchip) technology which greatly the reduced size and cost of their mainframe predecessors. Then, after "chip-on-a-chip" was commercialized, the cost to manufacture a computer system again dropped dramatically. Arithmetic, logic and control functions that had previously occupied several costly circuit boards became available in a single integrated circuit which made high-volume manufacture possible. Concurrently, solid state memory advancements eliminated bulky, costly and power-hungry magnetic core systems used in previous generations.

Early advancements were generally created by independent

entities and led to the availability of cheap, fast computing and affordable disk storage. Within only a decade, computers became common consumer goods for word processing and gaming. Computing and information storage were contained in personal standalone units.

Speaking at a 1977 World Future Society meeting, Digital Equipment Corporation CEO Ken Olsen famously said, "There is no reason for any individual to have a computer in his home." His company reached its peak in the late 1980s as the number two computer manufacturer in the United States with sales revenues of $14 billion. Company setbacks were largely blamed on Olsen's failure to anticipate or understand a burgeoning computer market and led to Digital's desperation sale to Compaq in 1998...followed by a purchase by Hewlett-Packard in 2002.[4]

Personal computers increasingly earned their place in private homes and businesses by the late 1980s. Families, for example, found "kitchen computers" convenient for storing easily retrievable disk-based recipe catalogs, medical databases for child care, financial records and encyclopedias for school work.

Although predicted to be commonplace before the end of the decade, computers still weren't powerful enough to match more optimistic visions. Due to limited memory capacities, they could not yet multitask. Floppy disk-based storage was inadequate both in capacity and speed for multimedia, and display graphics were blocky and blurry with jagged text.

Networking technologies created in university computer sciences departments soon led to substantial collaborative software improvements. The resulting emergence of an open-source information culture then spread throughout wide user communities which took advantage of—and also contributed to—common operating systems, programming languages and tools.

It took another decade for computers to mature sufficiently

for graphical user interfaces to serve broad, non-technical user markets which gave rise to the Internet. Equipment and user costs dropped dramatically as data catalogs became maintained online and accessed over the World Wide Web rather than stored on floppy disks or CD ROM.

The global digital traffic infrastructure Internet formed as networks became increasingly more uniform and interlinked. Simultaneous increases in computing power and falling data storage costs rapidly expanded world-wide service markets. The Internet, which was popularized for personal email chat and business forums, also became a growing exchange mechanism for computer data and codes.

The marvelous confluence of networking, capacity and storage began in the 1990s. In combination with an open-source culture of sharing both leading and drawing from the Internet, it still remains in the infancy of a yet unknown evolutionary creature. It is highly speculative, bordering on pure fantasy, to imagine what forms will emerge years, much less decades, in the future.

Breaking Moore's Law

On the basis of computer capacity alone, a prediction was made by American engineer and Intel co-founder Gordon Moore in 1965. He noted that the number of transistors per silicon chip had doubled every year, and he predicted that the growth would continue over the following decade. By his estimation at that time, microcircuits of 1975 would contain an astounding 65,000 components per chip.

By 1975, as the rate of growth began to slow, Moore revised his time frame to two years. This time his revised law was a bit pessimistic; over roughly 50 years from 1961, the number of transistors had doubled approximately every 18 months. Nevertheless, Moore's estimates were broadly accorded great importance as virtual law.

Moore had based his prediction upon a dramatic explosion in circuit complexity made possible by steadily shrinking sizes of transistors over the decades. Measured in millimeters in the late 1940s, the dimensions of a typical transistor in the early 2010s were more commonly expressed in tens of nanometers (a nanometer being one-billionth of a meter)—a reduction factor of over 100,000.

Transistor features measuring less than a micron (a micrometer, or one-millionth of a meter) were attained during the 1980s, when dynamic random-access memory (DRAM) chips began offering megabyte storage capacities.

At the dawn of the 21st century, these features approached 0.1 micron across, which allowed the manufacture of gigabyte memory chips and microprocessors that operate at gigahertz frequencies. Moore's law continued into the second decade of the 21st century with the introduction of three-dimensional transistors that were tens of nanometers in size.

Problems with Moore's original capacity estimate surfaced in 1975 when the estimate encountered a technical snag due to limitations posed by the photolithography process. The process, used to transfer the chip patterns to the silicon wafers, used light with a 193-nanometer wavelength to create chips which feature just 14 nanometers. Although the oversized light wavelength was not an insurmountable problem, it added extra complexity and cost to the manufacturing process. And while it has long been hoped that extreme UV, with a 13.5nm wavelength, will ease this constraint, production-ready EUV technology has proven difficult to engineer.

A roadmap around chip limitations sometimes described as "More than Moore" applies highly integrated chips which combine a diverse array of sensors and low-power processors. With the growth of smartphones and the "Internet of Things," these processors include RAM, power regulation and analog capabilities essential for GPS, cellular, Wi-Fi radios and even advanced microelectromechanical components such as gyroscopes and accelerometers.

Computer chip technology advancements are applying new materials such as indium antimonide, indium gallium arsenide and carbon (both in nanotube and graphene forms) which promise higher switching speeds at much lower power than silicon. Coming soon, expect monolithic 3D chips, where a single piece of silicon has multiple layers of components built upon a single die.

Computer processing capacities are accelerating at an even more astounding rate with the advent of recent Quantum Computing (QC) advancements. As University of Maryland researcher Christopher Moore testified at an October 2017 House Science Committee hearing on "American Leadership in Quantum Technology," that merely 300 atoms under full quantum computer control might potentially store more pieces of information than the number of atoms that exist in the entire Universe.

Since first proposed by Russian mathematician Yuri Manin in 1980, QC progress now continues to advance at a rapidly accelerating pace:

- D-Wave Systems, a company based in Burnaby, British Columbia, demonstrated a special-function 16-qubit QC in 2007 at the Mountain View, California, Computer History Museum.

  In 2011, D-Wave Systems sold its first 128-qubit commercial system ("D-Wave One") to the Lockheed Martin Quantum Computing Center located at the University of Southern California. The companies have since entered into multi-year agreements which have led to the development of more powerful D-Wave Two and D-Wave 2X systems.

- In 2013, Google established a Quantum Artificial Intelligence Laboratory (QAIL) at NASA's Ames

Research Center at Moffett Field, California, in collaboration with the Universities Space Research Association (USRA).

- In 2015, QAIL publicly displayed a 10-foot-tall D-Wave 2X unit chilled at 180 times colder than deep space which is expected to operate 100 million times faster than any conventional computer.

- IBM has recently announced an initiative to build a commercially-available "IBM Q" along with an Application Program Interface (API) to enable customers and programmers to begin building interfaces between the company's existing five-qubit cloud-based computer and conventional computers.

In any case, there is no way to turn back the clock of progress where even Einstein's space-time continuum takes on a new dimension of meaning. Unlike the speed of light, there are no known theoretical limits to computational intelligence.

Whereas the computational power of the human brain is largely pre-wired by evolution, AI capacities arising from revolutionary computer technology power and applications are growing exponentially.

Something else to expect…Moore's innovative lawbreakers will continue to produce computing processors which are more versatile, faster, smaller and energy-efficient in response to ever-growing demands for smarter systems that both support and compete with human brains and enterprises.

AI that Mimics and Reads Our Minds

Will computers like the fictional HAL in *2001: A Space Odyssey* ever take on intellectual qualities often associated with lessons gained through human experience?

Yes. And they already are.

A technique called "Generative Adversarial Networks"

(GANs) trains competing AI algorithms to challenge each other, learn from mistakes and even to fool one another with convincing deceptions.[5]

GANs is an example within a wide-ranging AI technology field broadly referred to as machine learning which essentially mimics the way we learn from trial and error using positive and negative reinforcement methods to achieve the desired outcome. The process uses two opposing reward or loss functions: one a generative model (also known as the environment) and the other a discriminative model (also known as an agent).

In one example, a GANs generator randomly creates images that the discriminator must identify as either real or recognize to be an artificial fake. Both entities are trained over a large number of iterations, with each iteration improving the "skill" ability of each. Over time, the discriminator learns to ever-more reliably tell fake images from real images, while the generator uses the feedback from the discriminator to learn to produce more convincing fake images.

Another example of a multi-agent GAN is "Style Transfer," where the model is provided two photos and two discriminators are tasked to produce a single picture. One of the discriminators is rewarded by conserving the content of the first image, while the other is rewarded by preserving the style of the second image. In the case of one discriminator presenting an abstract pattern—and the other presenting a picture of an elephant—each will work hard to come up with a compromise which satisfies both. Applying loss/reward criteria, a single picture will result after perhaps millions of iterations.

Successful GANs applications for text still have a way to go. Jeremy Howard, a University of San Francisco faculty member, developed a bot which was trained to speak like Friedrich Nietzsche after being provided the complete writings of that author. After a large number of iterations, the generator started to speak in a manner similar to Nietzsche, but the sentences didn't make sense. While companies are working on language-to-meaning mapping, we are still a long way from being there.[6]

As for mimicking life-like voices, that's far more successful. The systems can learn to reproduce a given text string of realistic impersonations after being given about 20 minutes of voice samples.

Technological progress is also rapidly advancing AI-enhanced brain scanning capabilities which will enable scientists and snoops to track what we are thinking, to test our truthfulness and perhaps eventually to download our very selves.[7]

Although these technologies are enormously exciting from cognitive research and medical perspectives, they nevertheless also present a range of serious social weaponization risks.

As discussed by tech entrepreneur and Stanford University AI lecturer Jerry Kaplan, an emerging wave of cognitive technology raises deep questions about how our material brains form our intangible minds, the true nature of consciousness and the exercise of free will.

Such technologies can also be applied to overcome conscious free will. Kaplan points out, for example, that "enhanced interrogation" would become a thing of the past if investigators could directly query a suspected terrorist's mind to reveal co-conspirators and targets. He notes:

The world would have to decide whether such methods meet human-rights standards, especially since authoritarian governments would almost certainly use them to try to identify subversive thoughts or exposure to prohibited ideas or materials.

Full capabilities to read human minds still remain a while off, but the pace of dramatic achievements is quickening.

Although relatively crude by more recent standards, 1980s-vintage magnetic resonance imaging scans nevertheless made soft tissue of the living human brain visible at a level of detail that could only previously be observed in autopsies. This MRI capability provided medical professionals with invaluable therapeutic treatment snapshots of damaged and diseased brains.

More advanced and "functional" MRI, which came along a decade later, enabled researchers to measure changes in brain regions through a technique that detects oxygenated blood flow. This new process revealed both brain activity and structure.

Access to fMRI provided a window through which cognitive neuroscientists could not only identify which parts of the brain recognized and made sense of such special features of the outside world as different faces, words and smells, but also enabled them to watch thoughts dynamically rippling across regions of the brain.

These fMRI scanning capabilities are continually being upgraded to provide ever-greater precision. They have evolved from measuring resolutions ranging from accuracies thousands or hundreds of neurons down to goals of observing individual neurons.

AI machine learning techniques enable cognitive fMRI researchers to analyze huge sets of "big data" collected from enormous quantities of brain scan information to reveal subtle, hard-to-detect patterns of thinking which are common to most or all people. Current research indicates that some mental functions, such as experiencing fear or recognizing individual faces, appear to involve specialized sections of the brain. Other mental functions are more distributed and are simultaneously activated in many different parts of the brain.

Jack Gallant and his collaborators at the University of California, Berkeley, have used fMRI to produce remarkably detailed maps showing which sections of the brain react to different words and semantic concepts. The maps recorded changes in blood flow to each of tens of thousands of "voxels"— the units in a three-dimensional grid of locations in the brain.[8]

Gallant's team conducted an experiment in which seven volunteers listened to two hours of stories from "The Moth

15

Radio Hour," a popular storytelling podcast, while their heads rested in the custom-formed cradle of an fMRI machine. The researchers then grouped the words spoken in the stories into 985 categories, each representing some common semantic dimensions. (For example, the words "month" and "week" fall into the same category.)

Correlations of participant brain activities with words told in the stories revealed that the study groups' brains organized and processed the same word concepts in similar ways. Dr. Galant concluded from this that improved imaging technology will make it possible to "eavesdrop" on a person's internal dialogue, to the extent that they are thinking in words. He said that it remains only a question of "when" this will occur—not one of "if" it will happen.

Remarkable as these results are, they are likely to pale in comparison to what may be on the horizon with emerging techniques such as functional near-infrared spectroscopy (fNIRS). This advanced technique has several advantages over fMRI: It's faster, cheaper and more portable, so subjects' brains can be measured while they are engaged in common activities like exercising, interacting with other people and playing games.

On the downside, current fNIRS devices provide lower resolution and signal discrimination, and are confined to measuring only outer layers of the brain. Several companies already offer commercial fNIRS devices, including Hitachi, Biopac Systems and NIRX, and the technology is being tested at Harvard, Yale, and Stanford.

AI-augmented scanners can't yet transcribe our thoughts, but they are getting closer.

The first generations can already "pick our brains" for individual word categories and related emotional and attitudinal responses.

Next, we might expect them to put together sentences—and eventually maybe even decipher our ideas and concepts.

Combined with other psychometric tools, these devices can

provide friendly interviewers and hostile interrogators with information regarding what we know about a particular subject or incidence and whether our responses to questions they pose are accurate and honest.

One approach in assessing whether a suspect is guilty or innocent of a crime is to determine whether he or she is acquainted with some unique aspect of the event, such as its location, a particular weapon or the victim's face. Studies reveal that brain activity reacts to familiar and unfamiliar stimuli in measurably different ways. Accordingly, future crimes may be solved by a "reverse lineup" to determine if a suspect recognizes the victim.

At least two companies—No Lie MIRI and Cephos—have developed brain imaging systems that purport to tell whether a person is telling the truth by comparing a subject's differing reactions to innocuous "loaded" questions. So far, their claims of effectiveness haven't been scientifically validated and courts haven't accepted their results as evidence.

Although there appears to be an expert consensus that these techniques are not yet reliable enough for use in law enforcement, information of this kind could revolutionize criminal proceedings. For instance, while it may not be possible to play back a defendant's recollection of a crime as though it were a video, the technologies may be useful in determining whether they have memories of the crime scene or the victim.

Such memory signatures might play an important evidentiary role in future trials, just as DNA evidence does today. Far more ominously, those with malevolent interests and agendas can weaponize brain scanning proceedings to detect and punish individuals with viewpoints that deviate from authoritarian ideologies.

While AI sci-fi-style mind-reading tools aren't yet well enough proven for official legal proceedings, they may find near-term applications in domestic affairs. It may soon be possible, for example, for a person to determine with some level of confidence whether their spouse really loves them, finds them attractive or is having an affair.

Jerry Kaplan suggests that future prenuptial agreements might require a visit to a brain scan center at the local mall to answer some very personal questions.

Noting that incremental mind-scanning progress will result in applications, products and markets that will be as hard to predict as social media was at the infancy of the Internet, Kaplan warns that one thing is certain:

> Our legal system, institutions, rights and customs will struggle to adapt to a world in which our most intimate thoughts may be subject to a search warrant or become a matter of public record.[9]

Tyrannical regimes most certainly will—and likely already are—applying these emerging technologies for mass propaganda targeting and social control purposes.

As reported in The South China Post, some government employees in China are required to wear brain monitoring sensors concealed in safety helmets or uniforms to detect depression, anxiety or rage. Selected high-speed train drivers and other Chinese workers are required to wear the same while on duty to detect fatigue and distraction.

China's expansive development, use and global export of social monitoring and control technologies portend terrifying global consequences for all freedom-cherishing societies. Be aware that this threat has already arrived in your neighborhood and has acquired duplicate keys to your home and cars.

They got those keys from you.

WELCOME TO THE SMART CITY ANT FARM

BEWARE OF LITERALLY hidden costs of aggressively marketed "smart city" proposals to make our lives more efficient and safer through Internet-connected and centrally monitored personal, household, municipal and regional systems. Those same networked devices, and those who manage them, will be fully capable of tracking, scrutinizing and ultimately controlling everyone—at every place—and at any time.

Global populations, Americans included, are trading away more and more of their personal privacy for promises of increased convenience and security. Spy cameras are sprouting up on lampposts and rooftops everywhere, facial recognition systems can track each of our individual movements and Internet-connected "smart cities" are wiring private home appliances within municipal energy monitoring and eventual control networks.

A smart city goal is premised upon supporting better decisions about design, policy and technology on information from an extensive network of sensors that gather data on everything from air quality to noise levels to people's activities. Some plans call for all vehicles to be autonomous and shared. Robots will then roam underground doing menial chores like delivering mail.

So How Smart Will Cities Become?

We are promised that technology makes cities better, more livable, more vital and prosperous, more convenient and efficient…more "smart." But just what, exactly, does the term "smart city" mean?

As it turns out, there are multiple definitions, depending upon whom we ask.

The concept of smart cities became a buzzword for both developing new cities for future growth and upgrading existing ones. The idea isn't entirely new. It arguably dates back to the invention of automated traffic lights first deployed in 1922 in Houston and has morphed and crystallized into an image of the city as a vast, efficient robot—a dream of giant technology companies.

The modern movement stems from the idea of digital information and communication technologies (ICT) which obtain large sets of data which are transformed and applied to urban policies.

There are two dominant smart city perceptions. The first and most prevalent is one where the urban fabric and everyone in it becomes increasingly instrumented and ubiquitously monitored and controlled from "everywhere." In this case, technology is typically viewed as a primary driver of change rather than being relegated to only serving as but one means to move the cities higher on the development ladder. In this new language of "smartness," the emphasis is upon smart information, smart meters, smart grids and smart buildings which are rapidly becoming ever-larger parts of our everyday lives.

The second perception envisions the smart city's economy driven by innovation and entrepreneurship with the goal of attracting business and jobs and focusing on efficiency, savings, productivity and competitiveness. ICT's role here is to facilitate and streamline private and public initiatives. In this case, the idea of smartness focuses on a smart use of resources, smart and effective management, and smart social inclusion. Within this view, the ICTs are one component of the concept, but by no means its bread and butter.

There is a dichotomy in this picture: corporate utopian visions ("ICT will save us") vs. an academic circle definition which is more varied, diverse and complex. Nevertheless, the two perspectives have morphed to become applied interchangeably, an ambiguous and not always positively connoted mix of automated utopian fantasy lands overseen by robotic versions of George Orwell's Big Brother.

"Smart cities" have come to be marketed as a conveniently imprecise, rhetorical and ideological rationalism for technology reigning supreme over everything…a panacea for all urban ills. Promoters market ICT solutions as quick and effective ways to deal with all manner of urban problems: growing populations, climate change, environmental shocks and other urban threats, including local urban crime problems, congestion, inefficient services and even economic stagnation.

Such rhetoric, energetically promulgated by big technology, engineering and consulting companies, is predicated on the embedding of computerized sensors into the urban fabric so that bike racks and lamp posts, CCTV and traffic lights, remote-control air conditioning systems and home appliances all become interconnected into the wireless broadband Internet of Things.

Writing in *The Guardian*, contributor Steven Poole asks:

> And what role will the citizen play? That of unpaid
> data-clerk, voluntarily contributing information to an
> urban database that is monetized by private
> companies? Is the city dweller visualized as a
> smoothly moving pixel, travelling to work, shops and

home again, on a colorful 3-D graphic display? Or is the citizen rightfully an unpredictable source of obstreperous demands and assertions of rights?[10]

Critic Bruce Sterling says, "stop saying smart cities." He wrote in *The Atlantic*:

The digital techniques that smart-city fans adore are flimsy and flashy—and some are even pernicious—but they absolutely will be used in cities. They already have an urban heritage. When you bury fiber-optic under the curbs around the town, then you get Internet. When you have towers and smartphones, then you get ubiquity. When you break up smartphones into separate sensors, switches, and little radios, then you get the Internet of Things.

These tedious yet important digital transformations have been creeping into town for a couple of generations. At this point, they're pretty much all that urban populations can remember how to do. Google, Apple, Facebook, Amazon, Baidu, Alibaba, Tencent—these are the true industrial titans of our era. That's how people make money, that's how people make war, so of course, it will be how they make cities.

However, the cities of the future won't be 'smart,', or well-engineered, cleverly designed, just, clean, fair, green, sustainable, safe, healthy, affordable, or resilient. They won't have any particularly higher ethical values of liberty, equality, or fraternity, either. The future city will be the internet, the mobile cloud. And a lot of weird paste-on gadgetry by City Hall, mostly for the sake of making towns more attractive to capital.[11]

Whole new cities, such as Songdo in South Korea, have already been constructed according to this template. Songdo's buildings have automatic climate control and computerized access; its roads, water, waste and electricity systems are dense with electronic sensors to enable the city's brain to track and respond to the movement of residents.

In India, Prime Minister Narendra Modi has promised to build at least 100 smart cities. Dholera, the first, is currently an empty backdrop landscape-in-waiting due in large part to flooding problems which have discouraged private investment. Despite promotional arguments that the city was planned as a greenfield development to serve the "public good," peasant and farmer protestors who lost their lands angrily disagree.[12]

One of the most ambitious pilot projects of this kind was in Rio de Janeiro and involved constructing a large state-of-art Center of Operations operated by IBM. Branded as "Smarter Planet," it featured impressive control center dashboards to provide panoptical views of huge amounts of data.

Rio made the great investment into the smart system as a tool to predict and manage a flood response in advance of two huge events—the FIFA World Cup in 2014, and the Olympic Games in 2016. That purpose soon morphed into an enormously larger urban surveillance information gathering and processing enterprise. Quoting Rio's mayor, Eduardo Paes:

> *The operations center allows us to have people looking into every corner of the city, 24 hours a day, seven days a week.*[13]

As Steven Poole warns:

> *The things that enable that approach—a vast network of sensors amounting to millions of electronic ears, eyes and noses—also potentially enable the future city to be a vast arena of perfect and permanent*

> *surveillance by whomever has access to the data feeds.*[14]

The project has also raised many practical questions regarding whether and how it improved the life of its citizens and in what ways it made the city smart.

Urban researchers Milan Husar, Vladimir Oudrejieka and Sila Ceren Varis point out that Rio's smart planning demonstrated a variety of inherent modeling problems which bring together certain distinct aspects which do not always fit together, while simultaneously hiding other issues. For example, modeling of weather predictions for events such as floods and traffic congestion used hypothetical statistical probabilities instead of descriptive certainties which can never be known in advance.

The best that can be done is to produce a set of possible scenarios while accepting and accounting for inherent uncertainties. The authors write:

> *In practice, this means that city representatives can only use these scenarios as aids for decision making on the basis of personal, electoral or financial risk if to take preventative action or not.*[15]

A major risk of this model-based planning is that city governments become inclined to use the official-appearing "data from a distance" to justify further regulation and control over urban systems and populations. Unlike in the case of rational comprehensive planning in the 1970s, the current information technology-intensive approach has a greater chance of achieving the political agenda-driven objectives they are inadvertently or intentionally programmed to support.

They also offer cover for bad decisions. City managers can always claim, "It wasn't me that made the decision, it was the data."[16]

Chinese Checkers

A sophisticated new set of technological tools—some of them maturing, others poised to emerge over the coming decade—are destined to wind up in the hands of autocrats around the world. Their use will allow strongmen and police states to bolster their internal grip, undermine basic rights and spread illiberal practices beyond their own borders.

One particular application of AI—facial recognition—has now become ubiquitous. The technology has been beneficially used by the U.S. Department of Homeland Security, the San Diego's Police Department and others to enhance security at large events like the Super Bowl.

In the hands of autocrats, however, the technology has great potential for repressive use. This is already occurring, thanks to help from large American tech companies that are working with China to establish widespread public monitoring and social media censorship programs there.

China has launched the development of a vast facial recognition network which is planned to be capable of picking any one of its 1.4 billion citizens individuals out of massive crowds with nearly perfect accuracy. Their state-run Xinhua news agency reported that Nanchang police in southeastern China located and arrested a wanted suspect at a 60,000-person pop concert.

Chinese police deployed facial recognition glasses in early 2018, and Beijing-based LLVision Technology Co. sells basic versions to countries in Africa and Europe. Such glasses can be used to help identify criminals like thieves and drug dealers—or to hunt human rights activists and pro-democracy protesters.

In combination with this expansive surveillance initiative, China will implement a "social credit system" which will assign every citizen merits and demerits according to how closely they are observed to conform to official behavior standards. Although currently voluntary, the program will become mandatory in

2020.

Examples of demerit-penalized infractions are expected to include bad driving, smoking in non-smoking zones, purchasing too many video games, paying bills late, breaking family planning rules, posting incorrect information online, jaywalking, or walking a dog unleashed. Those with low scores will be blocked from booking domestic flight and luxury business-class train tickets, staying at premium hotels, purchasing real estate, getting hired, having children accepted to university programs. They'll even risk having their pets confiscated.

According to the plan issued by Beijing's municipal government, by 2021, the capital's blacklisted citizens will be "unable to move even a single step." [17]

Chinese authorities are priority-targeting and testing the powerful tools of facial recognition and big data to detect departures from "normal" behavior among ethnic Uighurs and other Muslims in their Xinjiang region, a swath of desert and mountains abutting Central Asia. Many among the roughly 12 million Uighurs, mostly a Turkic population, are being imprisoned in political indoctrination camps with purported aims of assimilating them with the country's Han Chinese majority. [18]

Xinjiang detention centers reportedly resemble those established through China's now-defunct "laojiao," or "re-education through labor" system that herded criminals and dissidents into work camps before it was abolished in 2013.

Represented by officials as "vocational training centers," more than a million detainees in the new camps—chiefly Uighurs—have been forced to watch videos about President Xi Jinping and the Communist Party, sing patriotic songs and denounce Islam.

China has also embedded more than a million party members and government workers, mostly ethnic Han Chinese, to live with Uighurs and other minorities for week-long stays in their village temples and homes to monitor individuals and families in order to recommend whom to detain.

In addition, Xinjiang authorities have collected biometric data, including blood samples, from all residents between ages 12 and 65, turning the region of 24 million people into a leader in efforts to build a national DNA database.

Although this repressive treatment of Uighurs has drawn an international outcry, some of the same totalitarian crackdowns have filtered to other parts of the country amid efforts to reassert Communist Party dominance over all Chinese society.

Some of the oppressive technologies and tactics applied in Xinjiang were first implemented in other provincial regions, including Tibet.

Thousands of Tibetans deemed influenced by the Dalai Lama, whom Beijing denounced as a separatist, were also forced into re-education camps. Many others had their passports confiscated. Exiled Tibetan filmmaker Dhondup Wangchen, who had completed a six-year prison term on a subversion charge, characterized his country as having become "the world's largest prison"—one blanketed with checkpoints and security cameras.[19]

Building and expanding upon that Tibetan achievement, the Xinjiang program created a police state previously unmatched both in scale and sophistication.

Many thousands of high-tech police stations throughout Xinjiang tapped big data analytics to collect and sift through vast pools of personal information—such as an individual's movements, banking, health and legal records—in order to identify potential issues of concern.

Security forces were greatly expanded with orders to "fight till the terrorists are stricken with fear." Police were availed with hand-held devices to scan photos, messages and other data in residents' mobile phones in searches for sensitive materials.

Expansive networks of security cameras were linked with police databases.

Thousands of small urban "mini-community centers,"

spaced about 1,000 feet to 1,600 feet apart, provided amenities including household tools, first-aid kits and medications, wireless internet and phone chargers—along with covert devices to extract data from those mobile phones.

Chinese officials are actively promoting Xinjiang as a model for developing countries. The program director has reportedly hosted more than 200 politicians from nearly 30 countries, including Russia, Egypt and Turkey, for a symposium on Xinjiang's ethnic policies.[20]

A political dissident in Harare, Zimbabwe, may soon have as much to fear as a heroin smuggler in Zhengzhou. The Chinese AI firm Cloudwalk Technology has sold Zimbabwe's government a mass facial recognition system that will send data on millions of Zimbabweans back to the company in China. Cloudwalk will then refine its algorithms and perfect the system for commercial export to other countries.

As reported in *The Washington Examiner*, China is distributing those same intrusive tools of surveillance and social control throughout Latin America with potential threats "surrounding the United States." Quoting Colorado Senator Cory Gardner, "China's goal is to displace the United States, and they can do that by wreaking havoc in the Western Hemisphere."

According to U.S. and regional officials, ZTE Corp., China's second largest telecommunications equipment maker, has played a key role in these threats, both in their country and abroad.

ZTE is known to have been helping the Iranian regime track dissidents since at least 2010.

Venezuelan strongman Nicolás Maduro's regime paid the company $70 million to create a database and payment system for a "homeland card" (carnet de la patria) for a social control program which is modeled after China's social credit system. The card, which is used to control access to food, cash bonuses and other social services, also serves as a political control mechanism, recording where users gained access food and medicines in a country with shortages of both.

Human Rights Watch reports that the homeland card may capture voting history as well. According to a July 2019 investigation by *Reuters*, the data that this system generates is stored by ZTE, which has reportedly deployed a team of experts within Venezuela's state-run telecommunications company Cantvu to help run the program.

China has also supplied other governments in the region with substantial surveillance capabilities which can be used for social control. Ecuadorian law enforcement officials have purchased a network of Chinese security cameras with facial recognition software.

Business is also booming for other Chinese surveillance technology companies. The global client list of one such firm Tiandy, a CCTV camera manufacturer and "smart security solution provider," includes more than 60 countries.

Evan Ellis, a Latin America analyst at the Center for Strategic and International Studies and a professor at the Strategic Studies Institute of the U.S. Army War College warns that if enough countries adopt Chinese technology, Beijing will be able to integrate the different assets into a transnational "incredibly effective surveillance complex" that reinforces China's political and economic influence.[21]

The Egyptian government plans to relocate from Cairo later this year to a still-unnamed new capital that will have, as the project's spokesman put it, "cameras and sensors everywhere," with "a command center to control the entire city."

Moscow already has some 5,000 cameras installed with facial recognition technology, and it can match faces of interest to the Russian state to photos from passport databases, police files and even VK, the country's most popular social media platform.[22]

Meanwhile, China also plans to upgrade more of its own

smart cities. In Yinchuan, for example, commuters can use a positive facial ID to board a bus, and in Hangzhou, facial data can be used to buy a Kentucky Fried Chicken meal.

And they're really only just getting started. Planned megacities like Xiongan New Area, a development southwest of Beijing, suggests the shape of future "panopticons." These "smart cities" will feature centralized systems of control across financial, criminal and government records, drawing on all websites, visual imagery, phone applications and sensors.

There's no need to travel abroad to have your face unknowingly appear on candid camera. New York's Metropolitan Transportation Authority has begun installing monitors to scan motorists' faces at bridges and tunnels connecting Manhattan to other boroughs. Five seconds after a car enters the crossing, its drivers face is processed and compared to a state database. Police on the other side are waiting to nab people for warrants, suspected felonies, parole violations, and terrorist suspicions.

As Gov. Andrew Como added, that's not all:

> *Because many times a person will turn their head when they see a security camera, they are now experimenting with technology that just identifies a person by their ear, believe it or not.*[23]

Surveillance of American citizens gained great momentum through the enactment of the Foreign Intelligence Surveillance Act of 1978, but it came to broad public attention only after the 9/11 attacks and the ensuing global war on terror.

President Trump signed an executive order in 2017 calling for facial biometric scanning of all international travelers through America's top 20 airports by 2021. The Department of Homeland Security is assembling a biometric database called Homeland Advanced Recognition Technology, and the National Security Agency scans and stores millions of faces on the web.

Facebook, among many other social media companies, also collects images of its users' faces.

Invasions by Brainwashing Bots

China and Russia are poised to use and export a new suite of AI psychological propaganda products and capabilities that will enable even second-tier tyrannies to better monitor and mislead their populations.

One key technology in this arsenal applies automated personality assessments to tailor messaging slants that micro-target population segments based upon their particular psychological, demographic or behavioral characteristics.

In a widely-viewed TED Talk in 2017, techno-sociologist Zeynep Tufekci described a world where "people in power [use] these algorithms to quietly watch us, to judge us and to nudge us, to predict and identify the troublemakers and the rebels."

This is enabling the tailoring of far more effective "influence campaigns" aimed both at domestic and foreign populations.

According to a *Wall Street Journal* report, Russia's Internet Research Agency harvested data from Facebook to apply this capability during the U.S. presidential race. Data harvested from Facebook postings was used to craft specific messages for individual voters based in part on race, ethnicity and identity.[24]

Facebook and Google are known to have applied micro-targeting algorithms for precision advertising. Google, for instance, labeled users as "left-leaning" or "right-leaning" for assistance to Democrat political advertisers in the 2016 election.[25]

The more powerful micro-targeting becomes, the easier it will be for autocracies to influence speech and thought. As some American companies lead the way, more and more government entities—including tyrannical regimes—are certain to follow.

Speaking at an October 2018 discussion at the Council on

Foreign Relations, former director of the U.S. government's Intelligence Advanced Research Projects Activity, Jason Matheny, cited "industrialization of propaganda" as a growing international threat. For this reason, he warned the U.S. intelligence services to beware of the "exuberance in China and Russia towards AI." [26]

AI-driven applications will soon also enable authorities to analyze patterns in a population's online activity to identify and target those who are most susceptible to a particular propaganda message.

Emerging technologies are also rapidly changing ways that autocrats deliver mass propaganda through the use of online "bots" (automated account messaging). For example, researchers at New York University found that half of the tweets from accounts that focused on Russian politics during and in the months after the 2014 Russian invasion of Crimea were bot-generated.

Similarly, the October 2018 murder of Washington Post columnist Jamal Khashoggi prompted a surge in messaging from pro-regime Saudi bots. [27]

Bot messages will soon be indistinguishable from humans online—capable of denouncing anti-regime activists, attacking rivals and amplifying state messaging in alarmingly lifelike ways. As Lisa-Marie Neudert, a researcher with Oxford's Computational Propaganda Project, has warned:

> *[T]he next generation of bots is preparing for attack. This time around, political bots will leave repetitive, automated tasks behind and instead become intelligent.* [28]

Neudert told the attendees at the International Forum of Democratic Studies in October 2018 that the same kind of tech advances that fuel Amazon's Alexa and Apple's Siri are also teaching bots how to talk. Speech-synthesis systems made by companies such as Lyrebird (which says it creates "the most realistic artificial voices in the world") require as little as one minute of original voice recording to generate seemingly authentic audio of the target speaker.[29]

The Chinese government has employed what's known as the "50 Cent Army" over many years, with thousands of fake, paid commenters posting online messages favorable to Beijing in order to distract online critics. In the future, bots will do the work of the current legions of regime-paid desk workers.

Advanced generations of "deep fakes"—digital forgeries combining audio with video imagery, are already becoming good enough to fool many listeners and viewers. On YouTube, one can already see an unnerving mashup of actors Steve Buscemi and Jennifer Lawrence and a far-from-perfect video made by the Chinese company iFlytek showing both Donald Trump and Barack Obama "speaking" in fluent Mandarin.

These increasingly convincing bots will inevitably work together with other new tools to let dictators spread chillingly insidious disinformation. Dartmouth computer science professor Hany Farid warns that explosive growth in the number of these weaponized fakeries will leave those playing defense "outgunned."

Farid estimates that there are probably 100 to 1,000 times "more people developing the technology to manipulate content than there is to detect [it]…suddenly, there'll be the ability to claim that anything is fake. And how are we going to believe anything?"[30]

Hidden Bugs in the Internet of Things

Legitimate personal and public privacy and security concerns arise from the comprehensively wired-together Internet of Things (IoT) where just about every electronic device now has some kind of shared connection. Examples are smart meters, thermostats, smart speakers, web cameras, fitness trackers, healthcare monitors and many kinds of child toys.[31]

IoT involves adding internet connectivity to a system of interrelated computing devices, mechanical and digital machines, objects, animals and/or people. Each "thing" is provided a unique identifier and the ability to automatically transfer data over a network. Allowing devices to interconnect opens them up to a number of serious vulnerabilities.

The Federal Trade Commission's National Telecommunications and Information Administration, a unit of commerce, warns that while there are many IoT benefits for customers, "these devices also create new opportunities for unauthorized persons to exploit vulnerabilities."[32]

Many of IoT hacks don't target the devices themselves, but rather use IoT devices to access laptops and other systems holding personal information such as name, age, gender, email address, home address, phone number, Social Security number, banking accounts and social media accounts.[33]

Security experts have long-warned of the potential risk of large numbers of unsecured devices connected to the Internet since the IoT concept first originated in the late 1990s. A number of attacks have made headlines, from refrigerators and TVs being used to send spam, to hackers infiltrating baby monitors and talking to children.

One of the key security problems noted is the impracticability of updating them when vulnerabilities are discovered. Installing new firmware on light bulbs or refrigerators is not something most consumers are used to, and many manufacturers haven't contemplated those processes either. This presents a serious vulnerability for consumers and businesses alike.

The National Telecommunications and Information Administration reports that although similar risks exist with traditional computers and computer networks, they may be heightened in the IoT, in part because many IoT chips are inexpensive and disposable, and many IoT devices are quickly replaceable with newer versions:

> *As a result, businesses may not have an incentive to support software updates for the full useful life of these devices, potentially leaving customers with vulnerable devices. Moreover, it may be difficult or impossible to apply updates to certain devices.*[34]

Common hacking targets include attacks against connected medical devices, home monitoring equipment and industrial control systems which come with hard-coded passwords or credentials that can be discovered quite easily. When breached, they often lead to larger home or business networks, offering attackers easy footholds for further attacks.

Adding to privacy risks, many connected devices collect information about their usage, environments and users, which is then used by vendors for any number of purposes. One FTC analysis discovered the presence of numerous third parties in apps connected to IoT health and fitness wearable devices which revealed medical search histories, along with zip code, gender and geolocation data. The FTC report said:

> *The massive volume of granular data collected by IoT devices enables those with access to data to perform analyses that would not be possible with less rich data sets.*

Trolling the Internet to Net You

More than 30 billion devices are expected to be connected and generating data to the Internet by 2020. Any organization or insider that can control, process and exploit this information to spy on others in the network will be weaponized with enormous social and economic advantages.

Information harvesting and processing is being greatly

enhanced by rapid advances in AI machine learning and data storage capacities. Added to this, companies in both the United States and China are optimizing new software chips that can scavenge and make sense out of what they wish to glean from the natural language information clutter applying algorithms that are loosely inspired by human brain functions.

Such new tools will soon make it possible for dictators to conduct surveillance as never before, both online and in the real world.

China's Ministry of Industry and Information Technology has announced expectations that it will be able to mass-produce neural-network optimized chips by 2020. Doing so will enable China and other repressive regimes to more efficiently collect and sift through massive data on their population's speech and behavior and quickly exploit whatever information they uncover such as assessments of loyalty versus the likelihood of dissent.[35]

Deep machine learning is now training computers to identify and interpret emotional context within blocks of text using natural language processing.

Facebook now uses these techniques to examine linguistic nuances in posts that might flag users who are contemplating suicide, and smaller companies are working to score individual social media posts based upon attitude, emotion and intent.[36]

Predictim, a California-based AI startup, scoured text postings on Twitter, Facebook and Instagram to develop risk ratings for babysitter applicants solely on the language in the applicants' social media postings. The company's automated assessment app gauged the individual's propensity to bully, to be disrespectful or to use drugs.

Although public exposure of Predictim's prying triggered a backlash, anyone who posts inappropriately private, improperly vulgar or naively unguarded information on the open media invites exploitation by salacious eavesdroppers.

University of Montreal Professor Yoshua Bengio, a computer scientist known as one of the three "godfathers" of deep learning in AI, recently described to *Bloomberg* his concerns about the growing use of technology for political control:

> *This is the 1984 Big Brother Scenario...I think it's becoming more and more scary.*[37]

But we shouldn't assume that the benefits will accrue only to repressive governments.

Bengio, who heads the Montreal Institute for Learning Algorithms (Mila), has resisted offers to work for any large AI-driven technology company that doesn't protect user data. He has expressed particular concerns about protecting the creation of data trusts—non-profit entities or legal frameworks under which people own their data and allow it to be used only for certain purposes.

Recognizing that there are many ways that deep learning software can be used for good, it also presents great dangers from those who abuse its capabilities. Bengio advises:

> *Technology, as it gets more powerful, outside of other influences, just leads to more concentration of power and wealth. That is bad for democracy. That is bad for social justice, and the general well-being of most people.*

The digital information revolution can be appropriately viewed and celebrated as a great societal liberalizer. Simultaneously, these new technological advances, which concentrate great power and influence in the hands of a few, warrant serious rethinking regarding effective means to guard privacy and intellectual property rights of all free citizens.

Privacy safeguards must include legal and technical instruments to protect organizations, social and political groups and individuals from privacy piracy by all levels of their own governments. This will require policies and procedures that carefully differentiate between uses for legitimate purposes (such as traditional law enforcement) versus to gain partisan or other special-interest advantages.

Balancing enormous advantages of free and open information access with prudent privacy protections will present ever-greater challenges which will evolve in concert with ongoing fast-paced AI machine learning and data processing evolutions.

As Jack Clark, who directs policy for the research firm OpenAI, warns:

> *[W]e currently aren't—at a national or international level—assessing or measuring the rate of progress of AI capabilities and the ease with which given capabilities can be modified for malicious purposes.*

Clark adds that doing so:

> *[I]s equivalent to flying blind into a tornado— eventually, something is going to hit you.*[38]

INVITING INTRUDERS INTO OUR LIVES

COLLABORATIONS BETWEEN ASTOUNDINGLY powerful Silicon Valley information technology behemoths and Chinese overlords of population surveillance and control portend dark omens which should greatly concern us all.

In the United States, as in China and other countries, spy cameras are sprouting up on lampposts and rooftops everywhere. Facial recognition systems can detect and record each of our individual movements.

Our automobile and cellphone locations are constantly recorded. Our online shopping and lifestyle interests are being tabulated and distributed to product and service agencies. Our smartphones can constantly eavesdrop and secretly pass along private information.

Facebook is exploring what the *New York Times* referred to as "creepy patents" that will track "almost every aspect if its users lives."

One patent application uses information about how many times you visit another user's page, the number of people in your profile picture and the percentage of your friends of a different gender, to predict whether you're romantically involved with anyone.

Another Facebook patent application characterizes your

personality traits and judges your degree of extroversion, openness or emotional stability in order to select which news stories or adds to display.

Facebook filed a patent application that reviews your posts, messages and credit card transactions and locations to predict when a major life event such as a birth, death or graduation is likely to occur.

Facebook will be able to identify the unique "signature" of faulty pixels or lens scratches appearing on images taken on your digital camera to figure out that you know someone who uploads pictures taken on your device, even if you weren't previously connected.

They will also be able to guess the "affinity" between you and a friend based upon how frequently you use the same camera.

There is a Facebook patent application that uses your phone microphone to identify the electrical interference pattern created by your TV power cable to reveal which television shows you watched, and whether you muted advertisements.

There are also a couple of patent applications that will track the following: your daily and weekly routines, to monitor and communicate deviations from regular activity patterns; your phone's location in the middle of the night, to establish where you live; when your phone is stationary, to determine how many hours you sleep; and correlations of distance between your phone's location and your friends' phones to determine with whom you socialize with most often.

But of course, they will never really use this "exploratory" stuff.

Right?

Hello: I'm Your Faithful Voice Assistant

Are Alexa, Seri, Cortana, or Google listening in on your bedroom conversations?

Just as our online activities, including emails, information searches and website visits are constantly being monitored and stored, uninvited eavesdropping voice assistants can do the same.

Whenever a user initiates a voice assistant request with a "wake up" word or phrase, such as "Alexa," "Hey Siri," "Hey Cortana" or "Okay Google," the device instantly begins recording audio clips which are processed for responses by the operating company's server. They have already been tracking our movements and can pretty much anticipate what we may wish to ask them based upon records of our previous requests and interests.

Just as our online activities, including emails, information searches and website visits are constantly being monitored and stored, uninvited eavesdropping voice assistants can do the same. Whether spoken or typed, the messages leave behind a steady trail of recorded snippets which reveal special interests, habits and preferences that target subscribers for related advertising promotions and other purposes.

As Comparatech security review website founder Richard Patterson warns:

> While users can take a few precautions to lessen the impact on privacy, there's no way to use a voice assistant and maintain complete privacy.[39]

Their human-mimicking voices sound very pleasant, and very soon, their interactive conversations with us will become virtually indistinguishable from fellow humans. So maybe be a little careful when engaged in what we may mistakenly believe to be our private telephone conversations. That "person" you think you are sharing secrets with might actually be a robotic HAL or HILLARY replica of your imagined friend with unfriendly intentions.[40]

Do be advised that we may be wise not to trust them to

hold those cordial conversations confidential. In addition to being developed to retrieve information, arrange appointments, provide directions, play favorite music and remind us of scheduled appointments, they can also be used to whisper our personal secrets to others behind our backs.[41]

Also be aware that the sound activation feature on your smartphone means that the virtual assistants are constantly capable of listening and recording, even when the device is not engaged in active conversation with the user. That capability potentially enables host companies or outside hackers to listen in to everything that is going on in our surroundings—even when we imagine them to be sleeping.

Because smartphones have become essential companions, their sensors stay close to most of us throughout the day and night—in our car cup holders, on our desks and dinner tables—and yes—also on our nightstands.

A "multilateration" feature on our smartphones also enables them to locate themselves via cell towers or an integrated GPS chip. This marvel, which provides access to map navigation, also enables retailers and others to profile establishments the phone owner visits most frequently, and even how much time they spend there.

As quoted in Science News, Maryam Mehmezhad, a computer scientist at England's Newcastle University, warns:

> Those sensors are finding their ways into every corner of our lives. That's a good thing when phones are using their observational dexterity to do our bidding. But the plethora of highly personal information that smartphones are privy to also makes them powerful potential spies.[42]

Smartphone cameras can be activated by hackers to spy on their owners. This can be achieved either by secretly installing software on the phones via physical access, or by using a more common method through remote security breaches.

Marc Laliberte, an information security threat analyst at network security company WatchGuard technologies, warns that:

> These devices should not be operational in locations where potentially sensitive information is verbally passed.

Laliberte also advises that limited access can help people from tampering with the system:

> Privacy concerns arise when someone other than the voice assistant's owner uses the device, as most devices can't distinguish between different people's voices.[43]

These omnipresent devices which are with us 24/7 can be switched on by uninvited intruders to record private information about our special interests, habits and preferences for targeting of advertising promotions and other purposes.

A great feature of smartphones is that their functionality can be expanded and customized according to personal interests by installing apps. The scary news here is that many apps are being provided by disreputable sources with the intent of helping themselves to a lot more of that personal information than we realize.

We might ask ourselves, for example, why a new game we are ordering requires us (in small print) to grant them access to our contacts, our GPS and our camera.

Google Play discovered and booted 20 apps from Android phones and its app store which could—without the user's knowledge—record with the microphone, monitor a phone's location, take photos and then extract the data. While stolen photos and sound bites pose obvious privacy invasions, even seemingly innocuous sensor data can potentially broadcast sensitive information, such as about what users are typing.

Some stealthy data thefts involve very large social media

corporations that use computer algorithms to track and pass on data culled from our private online information searches, conversations and transactions. This process occurs without awareness by users, as they didn't read the small print in service agreements.[44]

Nevertheless, all of our personal data is accessible to government agencies. The NSA and CIA can potentially have any information disclosed to them...whether it's legal to do so or not.

A 2018 Facebook-Cambridge Analytical data scandal exposed the fact that Cambridge Analytical had been allowed to illicitly harvest the personal data of millions of peoples' Facebook profiles without their consent. This data was used for political purposes.

Some personal data mining activities attach electronic markers known as "cookies" on user websites and apps, which are passed to advertisers based upon corresponding product tastes and interests to be targeted. It's difficult to define exact triggers because the activation data is transmitted in an encrypted form. Host companies could potentially have a range of thousands of triggers to kick-start the process of mining conversations for advertising companies. A casual chat about cat food or a certain snack, for example, might be enough to activate the technology.[45]

Sam Nichols, a blogger with Vice.com, reported a surprising experience following a discussion with a friend regarding mutual interests in visiting Japan while in a bar with their iPhones in their pockets. The next day, both received pop-up ads on Facebook about cheap return trips from Tokyo. That event prompted him to try an experiment to see if his suspected phone source might respond to other unknown activation phrase triggers.[46]

So twice a day, for five days, Sam voiced certain trial trigger phrases, such as, "I'm thinking about going back to uni and I need some cheap shirts for work."

Suddenly, virtually overnight, he began receiving Facebook posts about mid-semester courses at various universities, and how certain brands were offering cheap clothing. Another private conversation with a friend about having run out of data capacity led to an ad about cheap 20 GB data plans.

Facebook, WhatsApp and other companies have dismissively attributed the eerie feelings some may have about smartphones listening to them as merely an example of heightened perception...or the phenomenon whereby people are more likely to notice things they've recently talked about.[47]

Living in Glass Houses

Those same AI and Internet technologies that communicate our private data, both to intended and uninvited parties, are recently extending our security vulnerability to a new category of eavesdroppers...the interconnected "smart" electronic devices we install in our homes and personal workplaces to make our lives more convenient, efficient and satisfying.

Included are smart thermostats that manage our heating needs, refrigerators that keep track of our food inventories, surveillance systems and displays showing today's weather or our latest emails or news as we shower. Many of these elements communicate together, with our smartphones, and also with the Internet.[48]

Although connecting many platforms together into integrated "Internet-of Things" networks, it also presents a host of very real and serious privacy and information security hazards. There are numerous benefits from the combination of the Internet of Things (IoT).

The home is itself in danger of becoming a glass house transparent to makers of smart home products. The challenge is that most IoT customers are predicated on inviting these devices.

As observed by the former *Internet of Business* editor Chris

Middleton, many citizens are actively embracing a surveillance culture as they retreat into homes protected by smart security cameras and doorbells, home safety monitoring apps, neighborhood security networks and even private police forces (whose prime function is to protect wealthy neighborhoods from drunks, beggars and homeless people.

Middleton writes:

> *The qualitative shift in people's lives brought about by smart devices, homes, offices, spaces, and cities needs urgent attention, warns its report, because of the extreme diminishment of private spaces that will result.*[49]

The rapid rise of facial recognition systems, emotion and sentiment recognition/analysis and systems that constantly listen to us in our own homes—devices that are primed to sell us products—mean that our environments are becoming more intrusive. This affords a virtual open invitation for data breaching hackers, political troll farm campaigners, financial account identity thieves and swarms of other unsavory scoundrels.[50]

One typical form of privacy intrusion occurs when one member of a household spies on another. For example, when one partner in a broken relationship who is familiar with the connected system of devices and passcodes jealously continues to monitor private and possibly intimate activities of the other.

Such abuses can be executed from long distance apps installed on targets' phones. Even if the identity of the abuser is known, taking legal steps may be difficult. Local courts are only beginning to address ways to apply restraining orders to protect victims of electronic stalking and intrusions.

Some 29 million American residences contained connected, smart-home devices in 2017...a number which has been growing at a rate of 31 percent each year. This growth trend will likely accelerate as emerging AI technologies make it easier and easier to automate repetitive aspects of our daily lives—and as devices get even better at communicating with each other.

IoT privacy invasion is burning legal boundaries as our homes have also become transparent to technological snooping from the outside.

MIT has released details of an AI system that can "see through walls" and infer the location of people.

In a seminal 2001 US Supreme Court case, Kyllo v. U.S.— in which police used a thermal imager without a warrant to detect heat patterns from marijuana cultivation in a defendant's house—the late Supreme Court Justice Antonin Scalia said:

> *In the home...all details are intimate details, because the entire area is held safe from prying government eyes...We have said that the Fourth Amendment draws a line at the entrance to the house.*

Two U.S. states, Arizona and Washington, guarantee privacy in their constitutions, with both citing the home as a critical context:

> *No person shall be disturbed in his private affairs, or his home invaded, without authority of law.*[51]

So now that our voice assistants and their real employers and sponsors can know where we are and what we are doing pretty much all the time—does it really matter?

Each of us must decide whether all this attention causes us to feel more like global celebrities, or alternatively, as ever-larger targets of Big Data mining profilers, nefarious hacking profiteers and other privacy-invading peeping Toms.

Emotional Privacy Matters

Meanwhile, the rise of AI and Big Data-enabled facial recognition systems now add "sentiment recognition and analysis systems" that can secretly monitor and record our inner emotional life over long periods of time.

Are you currently depressed? In danger of a heart attack? Dozing at the wheel of your car?

Artificial intelligence promises to figure these things out— and more—through an expanding toolbox of emotional detection technologies (via facial data, biometrics and voice analysis), sentiment analysis and "affective computing"— computing that relates to, arises from or influences emotions.[52]

Machine-learning methods are enabling ever-smarter AI systems to measure our individual tone, tempo and other voice characteristics and compare them with stored speech patterns that have been identified as happy, sad, mad or any number of other emotions.

As reported by Chris Middleton in InternetofBusiness.com, a range of businesses, health-care organizations and government agencies are exploring new systems that can analyze the human voice to determine a person's emotions, mental and physical health and even height and weight.[53]

While the science of vocal analysis has been developing for decades, cheaper computing power in combination with computer vision in a recent field known as emotion AI or affective computing is gaining broad applications.

Middleton notes that the technologies are already being used by call centers to flag problems in conversations, doctors are now testing it as a way to spot mental and physical ailments and companies are starting to tap it to help them vet job applicants.

At the end of last year, CompanionMX Inc., a company spun off from the behavioral analysis firm Cogito Corp., launched a mobile mental health system called Companion. The technology was developed with funding from the Defense Advanced Research Projects Agency, the U.S. Department of Veterans Affairs and the National Institute of Mental Health.

With the CompanionMX system, patients who are being treated for depression, bipolar disorders and other conditions download an app and create audio logs on their smartphones. The patients are asked to regularly talk about how they're feeling, and the information is automatically transmitted to an AI for analysis.

CompanionMX regularly monitors smartphone activity to see if the patient is withdrawing from contact with others.

The Mayo Clinic conducted a two-year study that ended in 2017 to see if smartphone voice analysis was capable of detecting coronary artery disease (everyone's voice has different frequencies that can be analyzed). Mayo collaborated on the project with the voice-AI company Beyond Verbal, which used machine learning to identify what it thought were the specific disease biomarkers.

Many major car companies and AI companies are developing AI voice analysis systems to assess driver alertness and emotions. The new technology will use cameras to detect facial expressions such as a smile and microphones to pick up vocal expressions such as anger. The company's algorithms then also apply deep learning, computer vision and speech technology to identify emotions and state of alertness.

When, for instance, a driver exhibits yawning or other signs of drowsiness, the voice assistants might address them by saying something as simple as: "You seem tired. Do you want to pull over for a break?"

The voice assistant might also engage with the driver in a more active conversation to improve his or her alertness level.

Although these technologies are still under development, they could be on the road in a couple of years. The voice assistant "Dagon Drive" can already be found in its current form in more than 200 million cars produced by companies that include Audi, BMW, Daimler, Fiat, Ford, GM, Hyundai and Toyota.

A number of call center-intensive companies, including insurers Humana Inc. and MetLife Inc., have deployed Cogito's AI software as a way to keep their agents sharp and their customers happy. The system analyzes and tracks all conversations and evaluates hundreds of data points including speech rates and voice tones real time.

Repeated pauses before answering a question, for example, might indicate that the telephone agent is distracted. Raising of a customer's voice during a conversation might indicate frustration.

When the Cogito system detects a possible issue, it sends a notification in the form of an icon or short message to the staffer's screen, such as a suggestion to acknowledge the caller's feelings.

Voicesense is one of the speech-based AI systems developed to make employment applicant screening more effective. Reviewers upload video or audio interviews to Voivesense's cloud and the system analyzes 200 speech parameters, such as intonation and pace.

An employer can use the scores to tell if an applicant is a good match for a job. For instance, if an organization is looking to hire a salesperson, the system would identify a possible match with someone who was highly active and engaged in conversations.

Voicesense acknowledges that its models provide probabilities rather than certainty, and for personal privacy safeguards, they don't store any data; the tool doesn't analyze conversation content.

AdventHealth Orlando, part of AdventHealth healthcare system, uses another analysis system, HireVue, to help recruitment efforts. Candidates who meet basic job requirements are invited to take an online interview using HireVue.

The AdventHealth algorithm evaluates responses to interview questions such as tone of voice and word clusters. In addition, it also incorporates visual analysis, examining very quick facial movements called microexpressions. Applicants who score high are called in for interviews.

The research firm Gartner Inc. thinks that emotion AI may even spread to consumer products. By 2022, Gartner predicts, 10 percent of personal devices, up from less than 1 percent now, will have emotion AI capabilities, such as wearables that are able to monitor a person's mental health and video games that adapt to a user's mood.[54]

AI must overcome a big public comfort hurdle before it goes mainstream: In survey findings released last year, Gartner reported that 52 percent of more than 4,000 respondents in the United States and United Kingdom said they didn't want their facial expressions to be analyzed by AI. And 63 percent said they didn't want AI to be constantly listening to get to know them.

Annette Zimmermann, a Gartner analyst who wrote the firm's report on emotion AI, said that about two-thirds, 65 percent, of the Gartner respondents believe AI will destroy their privacy. She told the *Wall Street Journal*:

> *Talking about feelings in AI, I think that's even more personal and more reason for [people] to be skeptical.*

Zimmermann noted that the systems aren't perfect, with the best ones achieving little more than 85 percent accuracy.

Rita Singh, a speech scientist at Carnegie Mellon University, added:

> *It's not exact. And we don't know whether we will ever be exact. But it's getting closer.*

As a matter of fact, it may be getting far too close for our emotional comfort.[55]

Larry Bell

BEHIND SOCIAL AND ANTISOCIAL MEDIA CURTAINS

POWERFUL FORCES THREATENING free and open exchanges of public communications have infiltrated social media.

No, I'm not referring only to China, Russia, North Korea and Iranian mullahs.

Those threats are lurking in secret algorithms in the darkness of shadow bans and are hidden under Google censorship platforms.

Top tech executives, Facebook COO Sheryl Sandberg and Twitter CEO Jack Dorsey, were grilled during a Sept. 6, 2018 U.S. Senate open hearing regarding their companies' roles in intentionally stifling conservative voices on their social media platforms.

Alphabet Inc.'s Google was invited to testify but declined—leaving a third adjacent seat conspicuously empty.

This hearing topic should be recognized to be much larger and fundamentally more important than which direction any ideological bias favors—whether to the political left or right.

These companies, which hold monopolistic control over social media and search platforms, wield tremendous influence over our open access to *all* public and private information and opinion discussions.

Their status as corporate—rather than government—entities, entitles them to determine what we are allowed to see, what we are not allowed to see and from whom, entirely at their discretion. Moreover, they can do so without having to justify their specific-case decisions, or to explain their rationale.

In 2012, Federal Trade Commission (FTC) staff issued a report recommending a lawsuit against Google—which controls 90 percent of all Internet searches—for anti-competitive conduct. The commission, led by Barack Obama appointee Jon Leibowitz, subsequently voted against it.

We Respect Your Right to Agree with Us

TheWesternJournal.com has documented recent Facebook News Feed algorithm changes which disproportionately handicap the abilities of Republican members of Congress to communicate with their constituents, relative to Democratic counterparts.[56]

Facebook CEO Mark Zuckerberg had said the undisclosed algorithm changes planned by his company would focus on news from "trustworthy" publications that people find "informative." These sanctioned endorsements apparently apply primarily to liberal sources.

The Western Journal reported that Campbell Brown, a former anchor on NBC and CNN who headed Facebook's news partnership team, told attendees at a 2018 technology and publishing conference that Facebook would be ranking news publishers based on internal biases.

Brown explained:

> *This is not us stepping back from news. This is us changing our relationship with publishers and emphasizing something that Facebook has never done before: It's having a point of view, and it's leaning*

> *into quality news. ... We are, for the first time in the*
> *history of Facebook, taking a step to try to define*
> *what 'quality news' looks like and give that a boost.*

Based upon a very large amount of insider reports from media publishers, The Western Journal's analysis revealed that Facebook's definition of "quality news" evidenced a decidedly liberal slant.

The reviewers first assigned each publication a number between 0 and 100 based on Media Bias/Fact Check News, a third-party website that analyzes publishers for political bias and places them between "extreme left" and "extreme right."

Next, The Western Journal checked the monthly Facebook traffic for each of these sources using data from the global digital market intelligence company SimilarWeb and compared January traffic to traffic from February 4 through March 3, adjusted for the shorter time period. According to the available internal data, Facebook began rolling out the major algorithm change on February 6, which negatively impacted conservative publishers.

Following the modifications, Republican interaction rates on Facebook pages decreased 37 percent, compared with a drop of just over 27 percent for Democratically-operated pages.

After removing the 15 publishers with the least traffic from Facebook, the liberal bias trend became even clearer. Although 12 of the most liberal sites among the remaining news sources averaged only a small 0.25 percent boost, the 11 sites in the middle—which ranged from "left-center" to "least biased" saw a significant 12,81 Facebook traffic increase.

The 12 most conservative sites, on the other hand, lost a huge 27.06 percent of their Facebook traffic. Among these, only two benefited, while 10 saw decreases ranging from 3.13 percent to a whopping 76.49 percent loss at the Independent Journal Review.

Together, Facebook and Google, which control 60 percent of all digital ad revenues, have used their market dominance to undercut competitors. Facebook has arbitrarily blocked publishers from promoting factual and opinion content on its news stream by tagging certain ads as "political." Included are materials which are critical of socialist Silicon Valley ideals.

In September 2018, Justin Haskins and Donald Kendal of the non-profit Heartland Institute, created a website titled StoppingSocialism.com. They delivered a speech on the subject to a group of college-age attendees at an annual Students for Liberty event in Washington, D.C. in January 2019. The following month, Haskins posted a video highlighting the conclusion of that speech which called upon millennials to reject the radical collectivism of Karl Marx. Its message urged them instead to embrace principles of the Founding Fathers: Individual liberty, personal responsibility and free enterprise.

After posting the video, Haskins paid Facebook to advertise it, a practice he had previously accomplished on more than 100 occasions without issue. This time, however, Facebook pulled the ad, citing "violations" of an obscure part of the company's advertising policies prohibiting the inclusion of older versions of the Facebook logo.

Haskins successfully appealed Facebook's rejection of the ad, which initially ran for a few days without incident. Then suddenly, and without explanation, his Facebook advertising account was permanently disabled. Imagining this to merely be a glitch in the system, he once again appealed the ban notification.

It wasn't an accident. Facebook's advertising team responded that its decision to ban the advertising account was correct because, "We don't support ads for your business model" which "[doesn't] follow our advertising policies." That disallowed "business model" presumably referred to StoppingSocialism.com along with Haskins' other conservative Facebook postings.

Facebook's response clarified: "There's no further action that you may take here." The notification added, "Please consider this decision final."

Haskins appealed the ban repeatedly in February and March, each time explaining his assumption that the closure was due to the ad's anti-socialism material. Every contact brought exactly the same response from different members of Facebook's support team. All stated: "There's no further action that you may take here. We don't support ads for your business model."

After two months of appeals, Facebook finally provided their reason for banning the account: "Specifically, it was disabled for running misleading ads." Again, presuming that the response referred to the socialism video—the only ad running at the time Facebook banned the account—Haskins asked for an explanation regarding exactly what aspect of the video was misleading.

Facebook's representative responded: "[N]o additional details can be provided regarding the decision made on your account. With policy cases, we often will hold back the red flags we use to identify violations to help preserve the integrity of out [sic] internal processes."

Haskins' final communication with Facebook expressed his opinion that the team was banning him for his well-informed political views as an outspoken socialism opponent. In rebuff, he was told: "I understand why you feel this way, however this is all the information that we are abbe [sic] to provide. Is there anything else I can help you with?"

The lessons here?

It really shouldn't come as any big surprise that the Silicon Valley communication content police have no ideological problem with socialism. After all, the Universal Basic Income (UBI) concept lauded by tech leaders ranging from Mark Zuckerberg to Elon Musk is unmitigated socialism on steroids.

Nor, unfortunately, is there any momentous new discovery that right-leaning views are subject to special scrutiny as "hate speech."

More than 100 Facebook employees had previously formed

an online group called "FB'ers for Political Diversity." Their sarcastic website posting stated: "We claim to welcome all perspectives, but are quick to attack—often in mobs—anyone who presents a view that appears to be in opposition to left-leaning ideology."

No, what makes this Heartland video censorship particularly noteworthy is the dogged persistence of its creators in confirming what we really knew all along. Namely, that it can happen to anyone online who steps out of their partisan line.

Libertarian media commentator John Stossel reported a story about Facebook's blocking of a young Guatemalan woman who had also criticized socialism.[57]

Problems began a few days after Gloria Alvarez had joined with Stossel in creating a video titled "Socialism Fails Every Time" and gave a speech on the subject in Mexico City. Some "students" posted what she referred to as "Marxist and Leninist memes" proclaiming "Boycott Gloria Alvarez in our university! We won't let her in!"

Alvarez responded (in Spanish) on her own Facebook page:

> *My dear Mexican socialists intolerants: Thank you! for trying to boycott my event...showing that panic that you have for the debate of ideas. Given yours are so bad, that only with bullets they can be obeyed just like in Venezuela and Nicaragua. You demonstrate once again that you are the intolerant ones against freedom.*

Gloria Alvarez ended her posting with a defense of free speech: "Where words are exchanged, bullets are no longer exchanged."

Facebook then cancelled her account with a notification that she had "recently posted something that violates Facebook policies."

John Stossel asks:

> *What violated Facebook policies? Was it calling the*
> *people who demanded that she not be allowed to speak*
> *'socialists intolerants' whose ideas 'are so bad that*
> *only with bullets they can be obeyed'?*

The only Facebook answer Alvarez had received was: "For more information, visit the Help Center...(U)nderstand Facebook's Community Standards."

Fortunately, Alvarez has connections. A few days later she wrote to Stossel saying, "a friend of mine that has a cousin working on Facebook Latin America (helped) me to unblock my page this morning."

That's probably good news if you happen to be fortunate enough to have a friend whose influential cousin works for Facebook.

As for the rest of us, good luck!

Twitter and Google biases have also gotten heat for from inflamed conservatives.

Responding to accusations that Twitter discriminates against conservatives, Jack Dorsey admitted during an August 18, 2018 CNN interview, "We need to constantly show that we are not adding our own bias, which I fully admit is left-leaning."

Dorsey added:

> *But the real question behind the question is, are we*
> *doing something according to political ideology or*
> *viewpoints? And we are not. Period.*

Given all the Twitter tweeting traffic emanating from the Trump Oval Office, that's probably a very prudent business decision. Nevertheless, this doesn't explain why numerous scholarly and informative PragerU.com videos posted on Twitter and Google's YouTube were removed as "hate speech."

The rational for hate speech, as Facebook puts it, is "dehumanizing language."

Yet none of the 50 or so censored videos—with as many as three million followers—included violent, sexually explicit or hateful content violating Google's stated Community Guidelines.

YouTube's algorithms and "community" of users can flag videos as objectionable.

Although those guidelines require an internal review team to remove them, one of their central policing members, the ultra-left Southern Poverty Law Center (SPLC), has a habit of labeling virtually all conservative organizations and commentators as hate groups.

Google's transparently left-leaning tilt is impossible to ignore.

The company went all-in for Hillary Clinton during the 2016 presidential elections.

Company employees donated $1.6 million to her campaign, and Eric Schmidt, Google's Executive Chairman from 2001 to 2015, provided direct political data analytics support.

President Trump has accused social media companies of "totally discriminating" against conservatives. In one tweet he said:

> [T]hey are closing down the opinions of many people on the right, while at the same time doing nothing to others.

In a 2018 letter to the Federal Trade Commission, Sen. Orin Hatch, R-Utah, called for the agency to specifically investigate Google for possible antitrust behavior, which he called "disquieting."

Hatch wrote:

> In the past, Google has offered arguments that its conduct is procompetitive. But much has changed since the FTC last looked at Google's conduct

regarding search and digital advertising.[58]

Although Google declined to comment on Hatch's letter, the company said its search function is not used to set a political agenda and isn't biased against any ideology.

The FTC had conducted a previous investigation over whether Google had skewed search results to favor its own services. The agency closed the case in 2013 without bringing an enforcement action after Google agreed to stop certain practices, including removing restrictions on the use of its online search advertising platform.

The large public media companies argue that they offer popular and free services that face intense competition, which benefits consumers. Nevertheless, Francis Fukuyama, co-director of the Stanford University Project on Democracy and the Internet and member of the Knight Commission on Trust, Media and Democracy, argues that their protestations of neutrality have become ever more apparent over time.

Writing in *The American Interest*, Fukuyama points out that these companies have maintained that they are merely platforms that enable users to exchange information freely with one another, and they have no obligation to filter content for accuracy as do traditional media companies like the *New York Times*, the *Wall Street Journal*, *CNN*, or *Fox News*. They are supported in this position by Section 230 of the Communications Decency Act of 1996 which was put in place both to protect freedom of speech and to promote growth and innovation in the tech sector.[59]

The central premise is that communication exchange platforms are very different from traditional media companies that are expected to curate the materials they publish by setting certain standards for fact-checking and journalistic quality.

Some of the most important decisions they render in this regard pertain to what information they deem fit to publish in the first place. For instance, they can determine whether or not—and where—to place stories about desperate Syrian refugees, transgender discrimination or the travails of Central American mothers above the fold, or alternatively they can emphasize crimes committed by undocumented immigrants, Hillary Clinton's email server or political correctness on university campuses.

Here, Fukuyama stresses that most complaints about bias in the mainstream media are less about deliberately faked news, and more about selective reporting that reflects the ideological preferences of media companies like the *New York Times*.

From the very beginning, social media companies such as Facebook and Twitter—along with the general public—recognized a need to filter out certain kinds of content, like terrorist propaganda and child pornography. They accomplished this goal using conditions pertaining to their terms of use. Such positive public attitudes toward exempting media platforms from responsibility for monitoring other types of nefarious content began to dramatically change following the 2016 elections in the United States and Britain, and subsequent revelations of Russian meddling in the United States and other countries.

But there was even a bigger problem that those media platform overlords themselves were responsible for. Their business profit model, which was built on communication traffic, led them to craft their algorithms to actively encourage conspiracy theories, personal abuse and other content that was most likely to generate user interaction.

Facebook, which has displaced email as the central channel of communication in many countries, already essentially functions much like a public utility. Fukuyama observes that this condition points directly to the other big problem with today's social media universe, namely that the size of the dominant private company platforms like Facebook enables them to exercise government-like powers of censorship.

Urging that anti-trust laws need to be updated for the social media age, Fukuyama recognizes that despite relentless growth of large platforms, there is yet no clear solution as to how the U.S. government can or should break up their grip on power. Although the Internet age demands that much more attention must be focused on modernizing anti-trust laws, any answers must take international dimensions into account. He points out that since Facebook's monopoly power extends across many different countries, abandoning its free and open market influence by simply banning it, as China has done, is obviously not a good outcome either.

Francis Fukuyama concludes:

> Social media and the internet platforms have been a great source of free expression, debate, and political participation, as well as being the leading edge of an innovative American economy. But private sector actors can flourish only within the context of a broader democratic polity, and as such they have a responsibility to help maintain the health of that political system. This was something well understood by traditional media companies, and is a lesson to be re-learned today.

Hence, we, all American citizens—ideologically left, right and center—face a common dilemma. Daily deep state revelations demonstrate unacceptable perils of further extending government influence over our lives.

Paradoxically, it should also be similarly unsettling to continue to allow powerful politically-weaponized social media companies, unbounded by cherished constitutional First Amendment free speech rights, to unaccountably silence whomever they like.

There are no easy answers.

Dangerous Internet Connections

Gone are the days when privacy meant locking your front door. Thanks to the Internet, complete strangers from across the globe may now learn embarrassingly personal or predatory things about you and your children from unguarded Facebook postings. Thoughtless sharing of inappropriate comments, private pictures and other personal blunders refuse to either die or recognize geographical boundaries.

The information revolution is bringing people of different backgrounds from around the world into a global information super network platform which connects many thousands or millions of social networks located everywhere.

Underlying these social platforms lurk uninvited eavesdroppers, cyberbullies and even sexual predators...invisible people who seek to weaponize careless communications against ourselves.

Many people appear to be quite unaware or unconcerned that the information they share on Facebook, Instagram, Skype, LinkedIn, YouTube and other virtual communities can be broadcast to some very unsavory characters. This information includes lists of other users who share common age and interest profiles who then become targets for predatory social network pretenders.

With privacy concerns come security concerns, since the Internet has become ever more integrated into our daily routines. We rely upon it for safe and accurate exchange and protection of an increasingly wide range of personal and business information. Included are myriad data accessible through Social Security numbers, credit cards and banking account codes and passwords that travel between mobile cell phones and laptop computers.

Hacking and email scams known as phishing, for example, dupe people into providing their own personal data to a thief posing as a legitimate business or agency. They inspire trust by constructing official-looking bogus emails, pop-up ads and even websites, then send out emails asking for data that reveals unsuspecting victims' identities. Some phishing emails may even install software on victims' computers used to redirect them to bogus websites.

Other schemes enable hackers to enter prohibited areas of the Internet in order to hack into another computer network. Once inside, they can view documents, files and confidential data and use it for their own purposes. Corporate breaches can release huge data treasure troves.

Consequences of electronic identity theft victimization can be financially devastating, emotionally stressing and long-lasting. It can require many months, or even years, to resolve financial and credit problems. It may involve disputing an identity thief's activity in credit files and cleaning up and closing compromised bank accounts and opening new ones. If the thief used your Social Security number to obtain employment, you'd need to address this with the Social Security Administration, and quite possibly the IRS as well.

Someone who steals another's identity may commit crimes in their name, harm their reputation and cause loss of employment opportunities through damaging employment background check reports.

Some stealthy data thefts involve very large social media corporations that use computer algorithms to track and pass on data culled from our private online information searches, conversations and transactions without awareness by users who didn't read the small print in service agreements that they are doing so.[60]

Yahoo's owner, the Oath unit of Verizon Communications Inc., has been offering a service to advertisers over more than a decade that analyzes more than 200 million Yahoo Mail inboxes for user data. This data offers clues about users' special shopping interests. Oath has admitted that this practice extends to AOL Mail, which it also owns.

Alphabet Inc.'s Google, the most popular email provider with 1.4 billion 2018 users, reported having done the same, but has stopped scanning messages in Gmail for targeted advertising as of 2017. Google has reported that it stopped the practice because it wanted users to "remain confident that Google will keep privacy and security paramount."

While it is not publicly clear what triggers the tracking technology, the technique is legal, and is even covered in terms of the users' mobile app's agreements which many or most people never pay attention to. According to the 1998 Data Protection Act, a person has to actively consent to their data being collected and used for advertisements.

Writing in Openmind.com, Zaryn Dentzel warns:

> *Much of the time, people started to use social media with no real idea of the dangers, and have wised up only through trial and error—sheer accident, snafus, and mistakes. Lately, inappropriate use of social media seems to hit the headlines every day.*
>
> *Celebrities posting inappropriate comments to their profiles, private pictures and tapes leaked to the Internet at large, companies displaying arrogance toward users, and even criminal activities involving private-data trafficking or social media exploitation.*[61]

Thanks to the Internet, a complete stranger from across the globe may view your Facebook profile and learn many personal things about you.

Nude photos and other personal blunders refuse to die or recognize geographical barriers on the Internet. "Revenge porn" has become widespread. Nudes posted online, like drunk tweets and Facebook rants about an employer, can live on in infamy. New companies are being born that exist solely to clean up customers' online reputations.

According to a 2014 Pew Research Center report, technology in bonded relationships now encompasses even intimate moments. Sexting, or sending sexually suggestive nude or nearly nude photos and videos via cell phone, is practiced by couples and singles alike. In 2014, nine percent of adult cell owners had sent a "sext" of themselves to someone else, up from six percent who said this in 2012.[62]

An ironic Internet privacy paradox has come to exist among typically self-conscious teenagers who exhibit a reckless lack of privacy concern. Online, something happens which changes this behavior whereby even those who are informed about dangers of identity theft, sextortion, cyberbullying, cybercrimes and worse continue to share private information as if no personal risk exists.

Why don't they care? Writing in ScienceFocus.com, Mary Aiken—cited as a leading expert in forensic cyberpsychology—concludes that it is because privacy is a generational construct which means one thing to baby boomers, something else to Millennials and a completely different thing to today's teenagers. She explains:

> So when we talk about 'privacy' concerns on the Internet, it would be helpful if we were talking about the same thing—but we aren't.[63]

The privacy issue is particularly sensitive to minors. Despite widespread attempts by schools, parents and concerned private and public organizations to raise their awareness, children continue to behave recklessly online.

Dr. Aiken points out that just because teenagers don't have the same concerns about privacy as their parents and don't care who knows their age, religion, location or shopping habits, it doesn't mean they don't pay attention to who is seeing their posts and pictures. Instead, teens actively adjust what they present online. This all depends upon the audience they most want to impress:

> *Everyone is calibrated for a specific purpose—to look cool, or tough, or hot.*[64]

They may ultimately be "impressing" a lot more and different fellow social networkers than they bargain for.

A child or teenager who has an active Facebook page and an Instagram account, who participates in Snapchat, WhatsApp and Twitter—then also throw into that mix all of their mobile phone, email and text messaging—may reach thousands of contacts.

Altogether, this is certainly not an intimate group of friends, or friends at all in any real-world sense that they really know and care about one another. In fact, many of their true ages and identities may be entirely false.

Exposures to predatory Internet anonymity can be particularly dangerous for naïve and impressionable teenagers. One of the most pervasive risks involves "online grooming," a strategy sometimes applied to inspire false confidence in young contacts aimed at setting up secret meetings for such purposes as sexual abuse, child prostitution and pornography.

Predatory online grooming can also involve a "smart handling process" that starts out without a sexual approach but is designed to entice the victim into a sexual encounter. This is sometimes characterized as a "seduction," which entails a slow process of disclosure of information from a youngster to a user aimed at building a gradual relationship of trust.

Cyberbullying Can Often Be Lethal

Despite widespread attempts by schools, parents and concerned private and public organizations to raise their awareness, some children continue to behave recklessly online.

Adolescents and teens make themselves vulnerable to

cyberbullies and sexual predators by a naïve and dangerous desire to share intimate selfie images and texts. Consequently, cyberbullying has become increasingly common, especially among teenagers. Emotionally harmful behaviors include posting online rumors, threats, sexual remarks, a victim's personal information, unflattering recorded impersonations, body-shaming statements and images and pejorative labels.

Cyberbullying is easily accomplished. In some cases, it can involve continuing to send emails or text messages harassing someone who has said they want no further contact with the sender; or it can entail repeated actions aimed at frightening and humiliating the victim.

Young people who suffer from low self-esteem, along with others with mental disorders, are particularly susceptible to extreme levels of potentially suicidal anxiety and emotional trauma. This is largely because they are less able to filter out and separate nasty things people say about them from healthy realities.

According to Lucie Russell, director of campaigns, policy and participation at youth mental health charity Young Minds, young people who suffer from low esteem and mental disorders are particularly susceptible to emotional trauma:

> When someone says nasty things healthy people can filter out, they're able to put a block between that and their self-esteem. But mentally unwell people don't have the strength and the self-esteem to do that, to separate it, and it gets compiled with everything else. To them, it becomes the absolute truth—there's no filter, there's no block. That person will take that on, take it as fact. [65]

The impacts are inherently tragic. A 2014 study by the American Pew Research Center reported that bullying victims are between two and nine times more likely to consider suicide.[66]

The Centers for Disease Control (CDC) reported in 2017 that whereas family instability and substance use are important contributors to teen suicides, the role of cyberbullying is becoming an ever-more prominent factor. Suicide rates for teenage girls are growing at a particularly fast rate.[67]

Excessive time spent online also often distracts interest and attention away from confidence-building group interactions that build self-respect and self-reliance.

San Diego State University psychologist Jean Twenge wrote in a 2017 article in *The Atlantic* that teens who use electronic devices more hours a day are becoming increasingly anxious, depressed and thinking about suicide. She argues that this is because the so-called "smartphone generation" is less likely to have less face-to-face interaction with friends, which is crucial to mental health and development of social skills.[68]

Unlike traditional bullying, victims often don't know the identity of the bullies, or why they are being targeted. This can have wide-reaching consequences because the content can be easily spread and shared among many people to remain accessible long after the initial incident. Also, since the practice often operates using stealth, victims may have no way to avoid targeting or escape.

Similarly, youthful cyberbullies are typically too immature to understand or have sufficient empathy to care about the emotional and psychological impacts of their activities. They may regard their actions as merely funny pranks, and they are unlikely to be aware that their actions may have serious legal consequences. Bullying that is sexual in nature or involving sexting can lead to conviction as a registered sex offender.

Those who imagine that they won't get caught if they use a fake name fail to realize that such ploys are doomed to fail. There are many ways to track them.

Virtually Losing Touch with Relationships

Even if many people tend to be even more connected with existing and expanded communities through the Internet, is the very nature of those connections altering the substance and quality of interpersonal relationships?

Writing in PsychologyToday.com, Alex Lickerman, M.D., urges us to remember that while we may enjoy online relationships using social media sites like Facebook or Twitter, for example, the differences between these kinds of interactions and those with people in the physical world are vast.[69]

Lickerman points out:

> *As long as we expect no more from these online relationships than we can give, no reason exists why we can't enjoy the power of social media sites to connect us efficiently to people we'd otherwise not touch. The problem, however, comes when we find ourselves substituting electronic relationships for physical ones, or mistaking our electronic relationships for physical ones. We may feel we're connecting effectively with others via the Internet, but too much electronic-relating paradoxically engenders a sense of social isolation.*

There can sometimes be a tendency to use electronic media to communicate to avoid uncomfortable face-to-face topics and potential confrontations because it blocks us from registering negative emotional responses such messages engender. In these cases, we intentionally isolate ourselves behind the medium's poor ability to transmit empathy.

Dr. Lickerman suggests that the "emotional invisibility" we witness on the Internet explains much of the vitriol we witness on many websites:

People clearly have a penchant for saying things in the electronic world they'd never say to people in person because the person to whom they're saying it isn't physically present to display their emotional reaction. It's as if the part of our nervous system that registers the feelings of others has been paralyzed or removed when we're communicating electronically, as if we're drunk and don't realize or don't care that our words are hurting others.

Lickerman concludes that while the Internet is an amazing tool which has shrunk the world and brought us closer together, it also threatens to push us apart:

Like any useful tool, to make technology serve us well requires the exercise of good judgement. For whatever reason, the restraints that stop most of us from blurting out things in public we know we shouldn't seem far weaker when our mode of communication is typing. Unfortunately, typed messages wound even more gravely, while electronic messages of remorse paradoxically have little power to heal.

He continues:

Perhaps we just don't think such messages have the same power to harm as when we say them in person. Perhaps in the heat of the moment without another's physical presence to hold us back, we just don't care. Whatever the reason, it's clearly far easier for us to be meaner to one another online. Let's try not to be.

A 2006 article published by the Pew Research Center asks, "Does the internet degrade friendship, kinship, civic involvement, and social capital?" Even in those relatively early

Internet days, it posited that a great debate loomed regarding its positive and negative influences upon how Americans, in particular, relate to fellow friends, relatives, neighbors and workmates.[70]

The article points out that on one hand, many extol the Internet's abilities to extend our relationships—we can contact people across the ocean at the click of a mouse...we can communicate kind thoughts at two in the morning and not wake up our friends. Some prophets had predicted a decade earlier that the Internet would create a global village, transcending the boundaries of time and space.

On the other hand, others fear that the Internet causes a multitude of social and psychological problems which include a form of addiction similar to gambling. Nevertheless, unlike a recognition that one is "gambling too much," this is likely a poor comparison in terms of impact with the notion of someone "communicating too much."

The Pew Research Center authors, John B. Horrigan, Barry Wellman and Jerry Boase, observe that a more pervasive concern among psychologists and social scientists is that the Internet "sucks people away from in-person contact, fostering alienation and real-world disconnection."

The underlying concern is that people become seduced into spending time online at their home computer screens at the expense of time spent with friends and family or visiting next-door neighbors. Critics worry that relationships that exist on text—or even screen-to-screen on flickering webcams—are less satisfying than those in which people can really see, hear, smell and touch each other.

The authors argue that debate regarding the Internet's impacts upon relationships is important for four basic reasons:

There is a direct question regarding whether relationships in the Internet age will result in the same kinds of personal ties—in both quantity and quality—that flourished in the past: Do people have either fewer or more relationships? Is the ability to connect instantly around the world causing far-flung ties to dominate neighborly relationships? More broadly, does the Internet take away from people's overall in-person contacts, or add to them?

There is an associated question of whether the Internet is splitting people into two separate worlds, one online—the other, offline. Both those who originally cheered and feared the Internet assumed that their "life on the screen" would remain quite separate and distinct from their existing "real life" relationships. Now it seems that this is not necessarily the case. For many, the Internet has become an integral part of numerous and varied ways that they relate to friends and neighbors. This begs a question, "Can online relationships be meaningful— perhaps even more meaningful than in-person relationships?"

Another question revolves around whether people's relationships (both on and offline) provide usable help. Do they add to what social scientists refer to as "interpersonal social capital," such as providing useful information or emotional support, lending a cup of sugar or providing long-term healthcare? The authors point out that while it is easy to give information on the Internet and arrange for people to visit and help, it is impossible to change bedpans online.

In contrast with the nostalgic way many people viewed small-town pre-internet social communities "where everybody knows your name," the authors ask: "where do they find community now?"

Finally, the authors ask: "to what extent is the Internet associated with a transformation of American society from groups to networks?" Harking back again to mythological days for many when the average American had two parents, a single boss, and lived in that friendly village or neighborhood where everyone knew their names, evidence suggests that this traditional vision has changed.

North Americans are no longer bound up in a single neighborhood, friendship or kinship group. Instead, they tend to maneuver in social networks which consist of multiple and separate clusters. Where most friends may not know each other, and even more likely, neighbors don't know a person's friends or relatives.

Relationships have come to be widely spread across cities, states and even continents. Accordingly, instead of a single community that provides a wide spectrum of help, relationships have become more specialized, where, for example, parents provide financial aid, and friends provide emotional support.

As for time spent online reducing social contact, it may mostly draw away from time spent upon unsocial activities such as watching television and sleeping. The large amount of communication that takes place is often with the same sets of friends and family who are also contacted in person and by phone. This, the authors believe, is especially true for socially close relationships—the more that close friends and family are seen in person, the more they are contacted online.

The authors conclude on a positive, noting that the Internet is not destroying relationships or causing people to be anti-social. Rather, it is enabling people to maintain and often strengthen existing ties, as well as forge new ones.

FRIENDLY AND FEARSOME WORKPLACE REVOLUTIONS

IS THE INFORMATION Revolution weaponizing artificial intelligence to compete against our human contributions to workforce innovation and productivity, or rather, will it ultimately free and empower us to exercise even greater satisfactions and achievements?

Very likely, the answer is both.

As previously mentioned, there are lots of things that computers can already do a lot better than we humans can.

They're really great at crunching through huge amounts of data to find particular information, connections and trend patterns that we instruct them to look for. They can review detailed and nuanced medical and legal materials to assist assessments of complex issues that draw upon huge volumes of the most recent research and case studies.

They can translate what we want to know back and forth between an endless variety of written and spoken languages in real-time so that we can communicate with "alien" members of our Homo sapiens clan. In addition, they can speak to us in virtually any language to answer questions regarding where we are, the best routes to get somewhere else based upon traffic conditions, whether we're in the correct exit lane and how soon we can find the nearest gas station, restaurant and restroom.

Thanks to machine learning, AI algorithms can now even compete with each other to make the most profitable stock market bets for their corporate overlords. Others are relegated to performing excruciatingly repetitive and boring tasks without fatigue or complaint so that we can do the more fun and challenging stuff.

So where do humans still hold performance advantages over computers?

At least for now we continue to be masters of tasks that involve general intelligence in formulating a problem in the first place, instead of just solving one. And while AI is superior at crunching large data sets and recognizing patterns, such as reviewing legal documents, human lawyers and judges remain much better at critical thinking and applying lessons-learned.

We humans also remain better at interactions with fellow Sapiens which involve empathy in any personal counseling realm such as medicine and other healthcare professions. Whereas an AI assistant can answer factual questions, offering good advice or purposeful listening is a different matter.

Although there are no reasons to believe that artificial intelligence will replace the need for creative thinking, problem-solving, leadership, teamwork and personal initiative, workers everywhere will nevertheless need to rethink traditional notions of where they work, how they work and what talents and capabilities they bring to that work.

As history demonstrates, we humans are a very adaptable lot.

Sure, by 1997 the computers were already better than humans at chess and, are now better at playing at Chinese game Go, rated 300 times more difficult.

But then, most of us probably haven't planned to compete in a Go tournament any time soon anyway.

On the other hand (or hands), although machines have always been better at repetitive tasks, robots aren't very versatile in responding to needs that require physical mobility and versatility—those handsy multitasking responses to such activities as maintenance, plumbing and electrical work.

And as Kevin McCaney observed in a 2016 *Bloomberg* article titled "Where Do Humans Outperform AI?," while AI is superior at crunching large data sets and recognizing patterns—the kind of tasks reviewing legal documents could involve—humans are still much better at critical thinking and applying lessons learned.[71]

Human doctors, lawyers and judges will decide what to do with all that AI research.

McCaney points out that empathetic human interactions involving teaching and counseling are another area where humans, as you might expect, hold sway. For example, while AI, like other programs, could prove to be a valuable teacher's aid, it can't replace a teacher, even the most boring ones.

An AI assistant can answer narrowly focused factual questions, recommend restaurants and supposedly find you a date, but good advice or purposeful listening is another matter.

Although AI natural language processing can enable algorithm-driven systems to sound human when communicating, the thought behind those words is lacking, which is evident when it comes to creative forms of communicating.

Kevin McCaney believes that we humans aren't likely to ever become obsolete after all. He writes:

> *AI can do certain things better than humans, but so can a blender. The fear of a world ruled by machines might someday be realized, but they're still machines, best viewed as tools that can help humans do their own jobs better, and little more.*

Nevertheless, AI is rapidly getting smarter about ways to impact our lives in major ways that were unimaginable until very recently. Since we human folks are the ones responsible for developing and applying AI to serve our own purposes, we might hope and expect that most of this is all for the good.

After all, who can argue against the facts that world-wide AI-driven Internet and mobile telephone connections, medical care advancements, manufacturing and agricultural production economies and access to online shopping bargains haven't provided some big-time improvements?

Consider, for example, that while farmers and ranchers used to make up over 50 percent of the U.S. workforce, they now represent less than 2.5 percent of this sector. Yet, more food than ever is being produced in America due to the automation in those industries.[72]

At the same time, what about those who worry that this AI revolution is producing technological revolutionaries who are already competing with our brains and physical dexterity for employment, economic compensation and our pride of self-worth? These include flesh and bleeding sorts of people who argue that the resulting losses of industries and jobs destroyed through the "disruption" component of AI may often outweigh the benefits of the creation.

So, let's look back at similar concerns and consequences of some previous revolutions.

Some Earlier Revolutionary Lessons

The "first industrial revolution" (along with even earlier agricultural and scientific revolutions) was both socially disruptive and forever transformative.

Conditions in Western Europe at the time when that rapid transition to a less human labor-intensive mechanized society present conflicted circumstances. Some bring to mind prevalent images of urban landscapes dominated by smoking chimneys and the sad plight of exploited coal miners sweating in the bowels of the earth. Others witness a dramatic overall increase in public health, longevity and food abundance.

The mechanization movement which began in about 1750 first impacted British lace and hosiery workers, then rapidly spread to other areas of the textile industry.

By 1811, angry mobs of newly unemployed weavers and other workers turned their animosity towards attacking machinery and factories that had taken their jobs. Riots by self-identified Luddites, supposedly followers of Ned Ludd, a mythical folklore figure, often turned violent. Many were arrested by British militia troops hired to protect industry, tried and jailed. Some were even hanged.

Unrest also occurred in other mechanized industry sectors. In the 1830s, for example, agricultural laborers in southern Britain destroyed threshing machines and burned hay bales.

Nevertheless, despite very real and painful employment disruptions and workforce shifts, the Industrial Revolution created far more jobs than casualties. The abundance of more affordable products in combination with rapid increases in general consumer prosperity gave birth to a new capitalistic era of entrepreneurship, innovation and global commerce.

Liberalization of trade from an expanding merchant base allowed Britain to produce and use emerging scientific and technological developments more effectively than countries with stronger monarchies, particularly China and Russia.

Some economists, such as Robert E. Lucas, Jr., say that the real impact of the Industrial Revolution was that "for the first time in history, the living standards of the masses of ordinary people have begun to undergo sustained growth...nothing remotely like this economic behavior is mentioned by the classical economists, even as a theoretical possibility." [73]

The Industrial Revolution was the first period in history during which there was a simultaneous increase in both population and per capita income.

During the Industrial Revolution, life expectancy increased dramatically. The percentage of children born in London who died before the age of five decreased from 74.5 percent in 1730—to 31.8 percent in 1810-1829.[74]

Until about 1750, in part due to malnutrition, life expectancy in France was about 35 years and about 40 years in Britain. The U.S. population at the time was adequately fed, much taller on average and had a life expectancy of 45-50 years.

A very major contribution of the Industrial Revolution was to food abundance essential to nourish growing populations over the past 200 years, constituting what can legitimately be termed a Second Agricultural Revolution.

As writer Yuval Noah Harari points out:

> *Machines such as tractors began to undertake tasks that were previously performed by muscle power, or not performed at all. Fields and animals became vastly more productive thanks to artificial fertilizers, industrial insecticides and an arsenal of hormones and medications. Refrigerators, ships and airplanes have made it possible to store produce for months, and transport it quickly and cheaply to the other side of the world. Europeans began to dine on fresh Argentine beef and Japanese sushi.*[75]

Harari and others also appropriately argue that while the growth of the economy's overall productive powers was unprecedented during the Industrial Revolution, living standards for many workers were very low. Histories of these early times bring to mind prevalent images of urban landscapes dominated by smoking chimneys and the sad plight of exploited coal miners sweating in the bowels of the earth.

Living standards and health gradually, yet dramatically, improved during the 19th and 20th centuries. Labor laws, for example, addressed exploitive working conditions and compensation practices; public health acts regulated industrial sewage disposal.

And while new and more efficient machines and processes of the Industrial Revolution yielded an explosion in human productivity, for a great many—craft and farm workers in particular—it cost them their jobs and livelihoods.

Philosopher Karl Marx had predicted that capitalism would be overthrown by communism so that oppressed workers would finally be free. History didn't turn out that way.

Karl Marx got it exactly backwards.

Equal Opportunity Role Disruptions

Endowed with human qualities of general intelligence and empathy, we should attach credence and concern for modern-day technological "Luddites" who are in real danger of being displaced by digital know-it-all human impersonators and mindless automatons.

Like, for example: android algorithms that respond to customer-service inquiries; chatbots that take fast food orders; tireless heavy-duty and precision manufacturing robots; cars (and trucks) that drive themselves; drones that deliver packages; and machines that instantly and accurately screen, diagnose and prescribe medical information.

University of Melbourne, Australia, computing and information systems Professor Justin Zobel directs our attention to a phenomenon whereby AI evolution is simultaneously advancing as multiple revolutions on separate, diverse and evolutionary tracks. He writes:

> *Each wave of new computational technology has tended to lead to new kinds of systems, new ways of creating tools, new forms of data, and so on, which have often overturned their predecessors. What has seemed to be evolution is, in some ways, a series of revolutions.*[76]

Zobel alerts us to a new AI reality that computers are not only influencing a reinvention of ourselves, but also rapidly evolving towards a capacity to reinvent themselves. Here, he urges us to recognize that computing influences upon human activities and society often characterized as "digital disruption" are also disrupting the very nature and future of digital computing.

This technological explosion of computational capacities and applications is more than a single chain process of innovation which has traditionally been a hallmark of other physical technologies that shape our world.

Zobel cites as a previous example a chain of inspiration from the waterwheel to the steam engine to the internal combustion engine. Underlying this is a process of enablement...the industry of steam engine construction yielded the skills, materials and tools used in the construction of the first internal combustion engines.

A big and consequential difference here is that in computing, something richer is happening where new technologies emerge...often not only replacing their predecessors, but also enveloping them. In doing so, computing is creating platforms on which it reinvents itself, continuously reaching up to the next platform.

Zobel notes, for example, that while computers were initially used in weather forecasting as no more than an efficient way to assemble observations and do calculations, today our understanding of weather is almost entirely mediated by computational models.

Another example relates to sweeping influences upon biological sciences and commercialization. For instance, whereas e-research was once done entirely in the lab (or in the wild) and then captured in a model, it now often begins in a predictive model, which then determines what might be explored in the real world.[77]

Wall Street Journal technology columnist Christopher Mims warns that these new advancements will have profound economic implications—for jobs, infrastructure, investment, global competition and more.[78]

Writing in a November 18, 2018, Mims notes that the first three industrial revolutions were driven by steam, then electricity and the automobile, then computing. These revolutions are generally recognized to include: (1) a shift from reliance on animals and human effort for energy to the use of fossil fuels; (2) breakthroughs in forms of electricity distribution and both wired and wireless communications; and (3) rapid development of digital systems, communication and computing power.

Mims believes that we may now be witnessing the rise of the fourth industrial revolution: an economy powered by the mobile Internet, automation and artificial intelligence. And whereas each of the first three are easier to measure in hindsight—tons of steel produced, number of automobiles on the road and the proportions of homes with a personal computer—it's far too early to know where this one will culminate. He writes:

> *Since it's just the start of the latest transformation, we can only try to find clues to the future by looking at the trends of the past decade, with the rise of the smartphone, the Internet of Things and cloud computing.*[79]

This fourth industrial revolution is evidenced by a sudden ramp-up of technologies ranging from phone components to wireless networks to wireless centers and points to a new kind of automation, more pervasive and smarter than ever before seen. This revolution will affect every industry—not just manufacturing, logistics or transportation—and is unique in the degree to which it is affecting white-collar workers. Mims projects:

We're either witnessing the end of work as we know it or 'merely' a profound transformation of what jobs humans do. Either way, the economic and political ramifications are likely to be on a par with the impact of the past 50 years of outsourcing and globalization.

The advancements are occurring in fits and starts. Mims observes that some trends are taking off in ways few have realized, like the population of industrial robots, while others are showing signs of leveling-off in recent years following preceding surges.

Just as Justin Zobel opined, each new advancement trend stimulates new opportunities and innovations. The explosion of smartphones, for instance, has created a need to develop a variety of new software ranging from apps to AI. New AI platforms (such as cloud computing and blockchain e-currency trading) have driven demands for more powerful networks (first 4G and soon its successor 5G). These large markets have, in turn, driven down the costs of an ever-expanding array of components that were once prohibitively expensive (all manner of sensors and cameras).

Mims concludes that this fourth industrialization will be an equal opportunity white and blue-collar role disruptor and economic catalyst. He argues that while exploding growth of the smartphone and cloud economy has brought automation to a sector that has traditionally been shielded from its effects— knowledge work—this is ultimately less about replacing workers than enhancing their abilities.

Automating such tasks as sifting through large amounts of data provides office professionals and entrepreneurs with access to better intellectual tools such as predictive analysis. In doing so, AI-driven automation also incentivizes demands and inventions of new jobs: data scientists and drone operators, for example.

Christopher Mims observes that combining mobile, the

cloud and automation with commerce is dramatically impacting many blue-collar jobs as well. One example is through influences upon the distribution of goods of every kind, both consumer and industrial. Included here are job transfers from physical retail sales to operations associated with distribution warehouses.

Although there are no reasons to believe that artificial intelligence will replace the need for creative thinking, problem-solving, leadership, teamwork and personal initiative, workers everywhere will nevertheless need to rethink traditional notions of where they work, how they work and what talents and capabilities they bring to that work.

As history demonstrates, humans are capable of adaptation. After all, we not only survived the first Industrial Revolution, but came out of it living better and longer than all preceding generations.

Yes, as before, there will be business and employment winners and losers in all professions. And once again, the Information Revolution will likely prove that we humans will leverage our innovations to provide better lives in a better world.

Big Career Winners and Losers

As computers continue to rapidly become smarter, fewer and fewer occupations we assumed needed us will be immune from competitive AI and concomitant robotic automation workplace challenges.

Businesses are racing to adopt AI technology, betting it will help them boost productivity and cut costs. Although what this means overall for the labor market remains to be seen, machines are certain to destroy some jobs that previously required human input.

Will the new jobs that emerge offset the jobs that are lost over the next decade and beyond? And if so, which kinds?

Some experts are skeptical, arguing that history shows that technological revolutions—while beneficial to workers in the long run—can force many into lower-wage jobs or unemployment in the short run.

Others are optimistic, saying automation always leads to higher productivity. This, in turn, lowers prices or raises wages, either of which leads to more spending and investment, which creates more jobs.

Many people legitimately worry that the resulting losses of industries and jobs destroyed through the "disruption" component of AI may inevitably outweigh the career benefits of the creation of new ones.

Still, others again more optimistically believe that while some industries and work roles will indeed fall as casualties of new technologies, they will be replaced by even greater, more satisfying and open-ended opportunities.

A 2017 McKinsey & Company report concluded that employment transitions to these disruptive technology-driven influences will be very challenging—"matching, or even exceeding, the scale of shifts out of agriculture and manufacturing seen in the past."

The study projected that about half of all global workplace activities could theoretically be automated, at least to some degree, using currently demonstrated technologies.

At least one-third of the constituent activities in about 60 percent of all professional occupations could be automated as well, although few professions—less than 5 percent—could be fully eliminated.[80]

A previous 2016 McKinsey Global Institute study estimated that between 10 and 50 percent of all U.S. job tasks could be automated using existing robotic technology. In about 60 percent of 800 occupations surveyed, at least 30 percent of those primary activities can be replaced by software. Some jobs, such as driving and working in retail and fast-food, may become entirely obsolete.[81]

Thomas Malone, founding director of the MIT Center for Collective Intelligence, believes that the AI technology revolution will fundamentally change the way that businesses are managed. His April 2, 2019, article in the *Wall Street Journal* predicts that this trend will lead to less rigid corporate organizational structures he refers to as "adhocracies" where non-routine activities and decisions fluidly shift between people with particular combinations of skills necessary to address whatever problems arise.[82]

Malone writes that while many peoples' primary AI concern pivots upon questions regarding which jobs will be eliminated and which ones will be saved, another issue, which is less frequently discussed but critical both to employee productivity and morale, is whether management structures will become more centralized and rigidly controlled or the opposite. Whereas the former condition will no doubt apply in some cases, this is not necessarily what to expect in others.

He asks us to consider the case of a traditional hierarchy—a factory for example—where large numbers of people are needed to do the core work operating machines and tasks that machines can't accomplish. Malone points out that coordination of the work of all these people typically requires layers of managers in centralized hierarchies to make certain that everyone does their jobs according to standard sets of rules. In other words, the sort of bureaucracy that has worked quite well for centuries.

For instance, in a traditional automobile factory without much automation, some executives and engineers decide on the product design. Lots of other people are needed in the factory to do all the routine work of cutting and painting metal, assembling parts and checking quality.

Several levels of factory managers are needed to be sure that the people are present, properly trained and performing their tasks correctly.

Malone observes that AI is dramatically changing this

picture. Whereas robots already do much of the physical work that was previously done by people, "in the not-too-distant future, it's plausible to imagine robots doing almost all of it."

We shouldn't imagine that robots can nor will become practical investments to replace human physical and mental resources in all businesses—including production and fabrication factories.

The McKinsey Quarterly dated July 20, 2016, lists four key business preconditions for such investments:

- Technical feasibility of automation.
- Cost of developing equipment hardware and software.
- Relative cost and availability of labor being replaced.

Other benefits beyond labor substitution including higher output, better quality and fewer errors.[83]

In their 2017, report McKinsey & Company researchers also describe types of activities that are most susceptible to automation. They attribute the greatest potential to physical tasks in predictable environments, such as operating machinery and preparing fast food. Two other important categories are collection and processing of data, which can be done faster with machines. These, they contend, could displace large amounts of labor—for instance, in mortgage origination, paralegal work, accounting and back-office transaction processing.[84]

The McKinsey survey found that since predictable physical activities figure prominently in sectors such as manufacturing, food service and accommodations and retailing, these are the most susceptible to automation based on technical considerations alone.

Accommodations for food service (first most automatable) include: preparing, cooking or serving food; cleaning food-preparation areas; preparing hot and cold beverages; and collecting dirty dishes. An estimated 73 percent of the activities workers perform in food service and accommodations have the potential for automation, based upon technical considerations.

Manufacturing (second most automatable) involves performing physical activities or operating machinery in a predictable environment. These activities represent one-third of the workers' overall time. Activities range from packaging products to loading materials on production equipment to welding to maintaining equipment.

Within manufacturing, 90 percent of what welders, cutters, solderers and brazers do, for example, has the technical potential for automation.

Retailing: Based upon technical potential, researchers estimate that about 53 percent of retailing activities are automatable. Examples include: technology-driven stock management and logistics, packaging objects for shipping, stocking merchandise, maintaining records of sales, gathering customer or product information and other data-collection activities. Surveyors calculate that 47 percent of a retail salesperson's activities have the technical potential to be automated.

Financial services and insurance: Researchers estimate a technical potential to automate up to 43 percent. Mortgage brokers spend as much as 90 percent of their time processing applications. More sophisticated verification processes for documents and credit applications could reduce that proportion to about 60 percent.

The McKinsey & Company researchers concluded:

> *Automation will have a lesser effect on jobs that involve managing people, applying expertise, and social interactions, where machines are unable to match human performance for now.*

Automation will also have less impact upon jobs in unpredictable environments—occupations such as gardeners, plumbers, or providers of childcare and eldercare. Not only are they technically more difficult to automate, but they are economically less attractive from a business perspective because they typically command lower wages.

On the plus side, the researchers conclude:

> *Workers displaced by automation are easily identified, while new jobs that are created from technology are less visible and spread across different sectors and geographies.*

Among the most difficult activities to automate with current technologies are those that involve managing and developing people or that apply expertise to decision making, planning or creative work. Often characterized as knowledge work, this type of work can be as varied as coding software, creating menus or writing promotional materials.[85]

Categories listed with highest percentage of job growth net of automation include:

- Healthcare workers
- Professionals such as engineers, scientists, accountants, and analysts
- IT professionals and other technology specialists
- Managers and executives, whose work cannot easily be replaced by machines
- Educators, especially in emerging economies with young populations
- "Creatives," a small but growing category of artists, performers and entertainers who will be in demand as rising incomes create more demand for leisure and recreation
- Builders and related professions, particularly in the scenario that involves higher investments in

infrastructures and buildings
- Manual and service jobs in unpredictable environments, such as home-health aides and gardeners

But what about the overall employment gain and loss numbers? Will AI and robotic automation be a societal net winner, or rather, a net loser?

The *Wall Street Journal* invited two well-informed individuals to present arguments their opposing views on this question in an April 2, 2019, tandem opinion article asking "Will AI Destroy More Jobs Than It Creates Over the Next Decade?" [86]

Carl Benedikt Frey, a fellow at Oxford University, presents the following case that history tells us the answer, and it isn't encouraging. So yes—at least in the short run—AI will destroy more jobs than it creates:

> *Throughout history, the long-term benefits of new technologies of new technologies to average people have been immense and indisputable. But new technologies tend to put people out of work in the short run, and what economists regard as the short run can be many years.*
>
> *More than two centuries have passed since the Luddites destroyed machinery threatening their jobs, and parallels are often drawn between the Industrial Revolution and our age of automation to suggest English textile workers were wrong in trying to halt the adoption of machines. While labor-force rates have trended upward since the dawn of the Industrial Revolution, the Luddites didn't benefit. For them, mechanization led to what historian Duncan Bythell called 'the largest case of redundancy or technological unemployment in our recent economic history.'*
>
> *The Luddites weren't the only ones whose incomes*

vanished. During the first seven decades of the Industrial Revolution (from 1770 to 1840), average real wages in England were stagnant and spending among low-income households declined at a time when per capita GDP grew 46%. The early gains from mechanization went to industrialists, who saw their rate of profit double.

Machinery angst erupted again in the 1920s when US factories reorganized around electric motors. Productivity data published in 1927 and showing that manufacturing employment had fallen since 1919 led to a series of displaced-worker surveys showing that many Americans had failed to find new work after 12 months.

More recently, wages for men with no more than a high school diploma, who would have flocked into factories before the age of robots, have declined since 1980, adjusted for inflation. Labor-force participation rates among men age 25 to 55 have fallen, as well. Economist Daron Acemoglu and Pascual Restrepo, in the study of industrial robot usage between 1990 and 2007, estimate that each multipurpose robot replaced about 3.3 jobs in the US economy.

Offering an example that many job-replacing technologies loom on the horizon, Frey notes that Google is building AI technology to replace people in call centers, and Amazon is building Go stores without cashiers. He writes that his personal research with Oxford colleague Michael Osborne suggests that 47 percent of U.S. jobs could be automated due to AI.

Acknowledging that "concerns over widespread technological unemployment are surely exaggerated," Frey proposes good reasons to be concerned about the short run:

First, the fact that robots have reduced employment suggests productivity growth alone may not be enough to offset AI-related job losses: workers will also have to depend on new jobs directly created by AI.

Second, early AI technologies might not produce big productivity gains right away. During the Industrial Revolution, early textile machines replaced many craftsmen without boosting productivity growth by much. It accelerated only after 1830.

Third, AI will give rise to new occupations we can't imagine today. But those jobs are likely to be highly skilled, and many displaced workers might not be able to do them—or move to where they are. Job creation and destruction has occurred unevenly across cities at a time when workers have become less geographically mobile.

Frey concludes:

For these reasons, we can expect AI to destroy more jobs than it creates at first. That would be the norm, not the exception.

Robert Atkinson, president of the Information Technology and Innovation Foundation, argues that no—AI will lead to more jobs resulting from increased investments and new spending.

He wrote:

It's time to take a deep breath and stop panicking about artificial intelligence and what it portends for jobs. No, AI won't destroy more jobs than it creates, No, the pace of technological change isn't accelerating. And no, we certainly don't need to tax AI to slow it down.

Automation, whether from AI algorithms or

computer-aided machine tools, hasn't led to net job losses yet, and it never will. It always leads to higher productivity, which in turn lowers prices or raises wages, either of which leads to more spending and investment, which creates jobs.

This has been true since Adam Smith wrote about more efficient pin factories in 'The Wealth of Nations,' and it will continue to be the dynamic going forward as things like ride-sharing apps lead to savings that people spend on other things.

Consider that from 1997 to 2015—boom times for information technology—productivity growth in EU15 nations was positively correlated with growth in labor hours, suggesting that stronger productivity growth goes hand-in-hand with more jobs.

To believe otherwise is to succumb to what economists call the 'lump of labor fallacy,' the idea that once a particular job is gone, the overall economy has one less job. It's this idea that lends to such loopy proposals as taxing AI-based robots to provide a universal basic income to sustain what doom-sayers assume will be a permanently out-of-work lumpenproletariat.

Reflecting upon history, Atkinson argues that just as the first Industrial Revolution benefitted most workers in terms of higher living standards, AI will benefit today's workers who, if they lose a job to automation, can more easily find another as AI fuels economic growth:

What's more, just as the IT revolution of the 2000s led to IT jobs growing 95 times faster than employment as a whole, AI will create millions of jobs building and applying AI algorithms and give rise to entirely new occupations.

Disputing Carl Benedikt Frey's projection that 47 percent of U.S. jobs were at risk of being wiped out by technology, Atkinson responds:

> *The second reason not to panic is that AI's impact on employment over the next decade is likely to be much less than what many have projected.*
>
> *It should have been noted at the time that the[Frey-Osborne] study wasn't an empirical analysis; it was an off-the-cuff forecast that made little sense in many areas. For example, does anyone really believe that fashion models, barbers and manicurists are risk—as Mr. Frey and Mr. Osborne claim—considering how incredibly difficult such occupations would be to automate?*
>
> *We should embrace AI and other tech-based automation as a gift to be nurtured with smart policies, not as a curse.*

Atkinson concludes his arguments for optimism by noting that AI algorithms will complement rather than replace jobs for many workers. For example:

> *AI algorithms aren't going to put your primary-care doctor on the unemployment line. No one in their right mind would ask, Hey Google, do I have cancer?*
>
> *[Instead] AI will give patients tools for things like measuring blood potassium levels via a smartwatch and it will assist clinicians in improving diagnosis. We will see similar benefits in other areas.*
>
> *To be sure, AI is much less likely to complement—and more likely to replace—less-skilled workers. But this should be seen as good news, since the US economy will have relatively fewer low-wage jobs—and relatively more middle- and higher-*

wage jobs.

None of this is to say the US shouldn't do more to prepare workers, especially lower-skilled ones, for transitions into new jobs and occupations. But those are manageable problems that policy makers can solve, rather than succumbing to a panic about a threat that isn't real.

Can anyone really predict how many jobs will be lost to AI-related technologies?

Researchers for the *MIT Technology Review* who surveyed projections by various groups regarding job losses (and some gains) at the hands of AI, automation and robots couldn't find any consensus. They concluded:

> *There are as many opinions as there are experts...prognostications provided by companies, think tanks and research institutions are all over the map.*
>
> *Predictions range from optimistic to devastating, differing by tens of millions of jobs even when comparing similar time frames. Many focused on losses in one industry...or results of a single technology such as autonomous vehicles.*
>
> *There is only one meaningful conclusion: we have no idea how many jobs will actually be lost to the march of technological progress.* [87]

In any case, history evidences that industries become obsolete and replaced for a variety of technological reasons.

Writing in Investopedia.com, Economic sociologist Adam Hayes optimistically posits that while some industries and work roles will indeed fall as casualties of new technologies, they will be replaced by even greater, more open-ended opportunities.

Hayes offers examples:

The automobile destroyed the horse and equestrian transportation industry. As the buggy makers and horse trainers saw their jobs disappear, many new jobs were created in car factories, road and bridge construction and other industries.

Elevator operators, once ubiquitous, were replaced by the automatic elevators we use today. In the 2000s film producers were replaced by digital cameras.

Eastman Kodak, which once employed many tens of thousands of workers, filed for bankruptcy, and no longer exists.[88]

Adam Hayes goes on to compile an incomplete list of industries that will be or already have been affected by this latest round of creative technology destruction:

Kayak and Travelocity have eliminated the need for human travel agents.

Tax software such as TurboTax has eliminated tens of thousands of jobs for tax accountants.

Newspapers have seen their circulation numbers decline steadily, replaced by online media and blogs. Increasingly, computer software is actually writing news stories, especially local news and sporting event results.

Language translation is becoming more and more accurate, reducing the need for human translators. The same goes for dictation and proof-reading.

Secretaries, phone operators and executive assistants are being replaced by enterprise software, automated telephone systems and mobile apps.

Online bookstores such as Amazon have forced brick-and-mortar booksellers to close their doors permanently. Additionally, the ability to self-publish and to distribute e-books is negatively affecting publishers and printers.

Financial professionals such as stock brokers and advisors have lost some of their business to online trading websites like eTrade and robo-advisors like Betterment.

Many banks are giving customers the ability to deposit

checks via mobile apps or directly at ATMs, reducing the need for human bank tellers. Payment systems like Apple Pay and PayPal make even obtaining physical cash unnecessary.

Job recruiters have been displaced by websites like LinkedIn, Indeed.com and Monster. Print classified ads have also been replaced by these sites, while sites like Craigslist have replaced other kinds of classifieds.

Uber, Lyft and other car-sharing apps are giving traditional taxi and livery companies a run for their money. Airbnb and HomeAway are doing the same for the hotel and motel industry.

Driverless cars, such as those being developed by Google, may prove to replace all sorts of driving jobs, including bus and truck drivers, taxi drivers and chauffeurs

Drone technology may revolutionize the way products are delivered, and Amazon is working to make that a reality. Drones may also replace pilots in a number of specializations, including those in the film video, crop-dusting, traffic monitoring and law enforcement sectors. For years, fighter pilots have been replaced by drones on numerous military missions.

3-D printing is growing rapidly, and the technology is becoming better and faster. In a few years, it may be possible to manufacture a wide variety of goods on demand and at home. This will disrupt the manufacturing industry and diminish the importance of logistics and inventory management. Goods will no longer have to be transported overseas. Assembly line workers have already been largely displaced by industrial robots.

Postal workers first saw bad news with the widespread use of email reducing the volume of everyday mail. High-tech mail sorting machines will eliminate even more jobs in the postal service.

Fast food workers recently protested to raise the minimum wage. Fast food companies responded by investing in computerized kiosks which can take orders without the need for humans. Retail cashiers have also been displaced at supermarkets and big box stores with self-checkout lines. Toll-booth attendants have been replaced by systems like EZPass.

Radio DJs are largely a thing of the past. Software now chooses most of the music played, inserts ads and even reads the news.

Educational sites such as Khan Academy and Udemy, as well as Massive Open Online Courses offered by leading universities for free, will greatly reduce the need for teachers and college professors over time.

Traditional television distribution is being upended by digital distribution outlets such as Netflix and Hulu.

People are dropping their cable or satellite TV services opting to stream online instead. Spotify and iTunes have done the same for the recording industry: people now choose to download or stream on demand rather than buy records.

Libraries and librarians are moving online. References like Wikipedia have replaced the multi-volume encyclopedias. Librarians used to help people find information and conduct research, but much of that can be done individually over the internet nowadays.[89]

Clearly, this is only the beginning of the beginning.

As David Roe, a staff reporter for CNS Wire.com and content manager for a number of U.K. software companies observes:

> In the world of technology, the mantra 'innovate or die' is truer for organizations than ever, and artificial intelligence (AI) is redefining industries by providing greater personalization to users, automating processes, and disrupting how we work. Like the adoption of cloud computing five years ago, the adoption of AI and the speed of deployment varies according to industry.[90]

Roe alphabetically lists some places where disruption from AI is already being felt:

- Agriculture: Industries such as agriculture, which are experiencing labor shortages, can experience automation and efficiency gains from AI. Few people want to work in this industry. Adopting AI and related automation technologies can be a matter of survival.

- AI Software Development: A combination of AI technologies like advanced machine learning, deep learning, natural language processing and business rules will have an impact on all steps of the software development life cycle...better and faster.

- Call Centers: AI may entirely replace the human-based call center industry. Companies are developing their own chatbots where users receive their responses in seconds and teams only have to respond to questions that were never consulted before.

- Customer Experience: Travel companies are using chatbots to create always-on personalized concierge-level services at scale...from airlines and hotels to travel agencies, AI is helping mitigate frustration during challenging travel situations by understanding the context of the customer's circumstance and providing contextually relevant options to resolve the issue.

- Energy and Mining: Oil and gas is one of the largest industry segments and a natural fit for AI. For example, the technology removes friction from port scheduling operations using a rare form of machine intelligence called cognitive intelligence (or human reasoning) to track tankers to determine when they leave port, where they are going and how much petroleum or LNG they are transporting.

- Predicting what is being shipped, plus refining destination and arrival times, helps traders make smarter decisions. This involves the fusion of the key cognitive capabilities of multi-agent scheduling and reactive recovery, asset management, rule compliance, diagnostics and prognosis to ensure seamless, autonomous operation.

- When machine learning is applied to drilling, information from seismic vibrations, thermal gradients, strata permeability, pressure differentials and other data is collected. AI software can help geoscientists better assess variables, taking some of the guesswork out of equipment repair, unplanned downtime and even help determining potential locations of new wells.

- Healthcare: AI has endless possibilities. For example, it is used to predict diseases, to identify high-risk patient groups and to automate diagnostic tests to increase speed and accuracy of treatment. AI is also used to improve drug formulations and conduct DNA analyses that can positively impact quality of healthcare and affect human lives.

- AI in the pharmaceutical industry can greatly reduce the time and cost of drug identification and testing. According to the California Biomedical Research Association, it takes an average of 12 years for a drug to travel from the research lab to the patient. Only five in 5,000 of the drugs that begin preclinical testing ever make it to human testing, and just one of these five, costing on average $359 million to develop, is ever approved for human usage.

- Intellectual Property: AI uses image recognition. This can apply 2-D and 3-D image recognition to provide visual search solutions which don't just scan objects for their likeness using data and codes, but through a combination of search algorithms and machine learning; the technology contextualizes and recognizes if one thing is visually like something else.

- IT Service Management: The AI-driven IT industry will

itself experience a disruptive change that will alter the way humans are involved in the service management process in corporate and government networks.

- The service sector use of IT will grow...particularly regarding the integration of AI-powered voice assistants to handle uncomplicated queries like establishing opening hours or determining when an engineer is due to arrive.

- Manufacturing: Industries dealing with complex knowledge requirements such as pharma and healthcare are particularly affected. Emerging applications focus on augmenting decision-making.

- Retail: Chatbots already enable retailers to dramatically increase the amount of data they can collect about the customer...giving them an advantage over those without them.

- Upgrades will enable chatbots to capture audible reactions, improve conversation capabilities and over time, provide analytics to the retailer that can be associated with the emotions and the mood of their customers while online. This will enable retailers to tailor and personalize customer service to encourage return business.

Tech writer Cynthia Harvey identifies five rapidly advancing and expanding AI-related trends that are altering the ways industries operate, survive and compete:[91]

- Big Data Management and Analyses: Enterprises are looking to AI to help them make sense out of their big data—especially their Internet of Things (IoT) data—and to help them provide better service to their customers. Applications include tapping into complex systems, optimizing advanced analytics and integrating machine learning technologies.

- Internet of Things: The Internet is also potentially exposing businesses to security breaches. Increasingly, IoT devices themselves are being turned into Distributed Denial of Services (DDoS) weapons.

- Augmented Reality: Retail companies using virtual stores are applying AR to lead customers away from brick-and-mortar stores to online purchasing. They also enable brick-and-mortar retailers to take virtual showroom experiences to another level, blending digital and physical shopping.

- Automation Consultants: IT teams are developing and tailoring automation software that autonomously frees up staff for more strategic tasks. Some experts, however, predict that AI will soon take over much of the coding work that AI developers currently do.

- Cybercrimes: Targeted espionage, ransomware, denial of service and privacy breaches present major and rapidly escalating trends that impact IT.

Robots as Companions and Competitors

Researchers at McKinsey & Company project that a growing employment need will for people with strong cognitive abilities. They also conclude in a 2017 report that workers of the future will spend more time on activities that machines are less capable of, such as managing people, applying expertise and communicating with others.[92]

Conversely, workers will spend less time on predictable physical activities and on collecting and processing data, an arena where machines already exceed human performance. The types of skills and capabilities required will also shift, requiring more social and emotional skills and advanced cognitive capabilities, such as logical reasoning and creativity.

The McKinsey & Company study determined that as a greater percentage of populations live longer, significantly larger new demands will result for a range of healthcare occupations, including doctors, nurses, nursing assistants and technicians and personal home-care aids.

Additionally, new careers and jobs will be created in technology development and information services. While this will be a relatively small number, compared, for example, with employment in healthcare and construction, they will more typically be higher-wage occupations.

Online skill training and secondary education programs will greatly reduce the need for teachers and college professors over time. It is plausible that children today will receive their undergraduate education largely online, and at much less cost.

In his March 27, 2018, Forbes.com article "Why Robots Will Not Take Over Human Jobs," business consultant and writer Andrew Arnold emphasizes that, above all, those entering the workforce today will have to be adaptable.[93]

Arnold wrote: "They'll have to be hungry for knowledge and committed to continuing education whether that's by taking an online MBA, attending conferences, reading books, consuming podcasts or taking advanced degrees."

Individuals must also face a harsh reality that the idea of a "job for life" is becoming passé.

Midcareer retraining will become ever more important for successful career changes in response to special skill mix demands. As technology moves forward, workers will need to develop new technical skills and keep those skills updated—including accomplishing this through on-the-job training programs.

Arnold concludes that although there will always be a demand for adaptable and versatile human labor, workers everywhere will need to rethink traditional notions of where they work, how they work and what talents and capabilities they bring to that work.

Whether AI will prove to be an overall job bust or boon, almost all professions can expect to experience transformative impacts. There can be no doubt that a revolutionary new AI and Internet era will dramatically disrupt many traditional career fields in ways that will favor some employment and entrepreneurship opportunities to the distinct detriment of others.

The ever-escalating pace of advancements in AI-driven machine learning and automation technologies, which already perform a range of routine physical activities better and more cheaply than humans, are also increasingly capable of surpassing certain of our cognitive judgment capabilities as well.

This traditional workplace disruption being an inevitable and inescapable trend, college applicants and their family mentors in particular are well advised to seriously think about which career paths are most vulnerable to obsolescence prior to investing lots of tuition money and formative lifetime years on inconsequential courses and dead-end diplomas.

Some disruptive, although not necessarily destructive examples of rapidly-occurring AI influences on some major business and career fields follow.

AI Impacts upon Healthcare

Dr. Bhardwaj, co-founder and CEO of Innoplexus AG, believes that as AI continues to advance, it has the potential to transform the future of healthcare in three critical areas: advanced computation, statistical analysis and hypothesis generation. Writing in Forbes.com, he refers to these general stages advancements in three waves of technology development and application:[94]

- The First-Wave AI: is composed of "knowledge engineering" technology and optimization programs which found efficient solutions to real-world problems...like using AI to estimate a patient's heart disease risk.

- The Second-Wave AI: is characterized by machine learning programs which utilized statistical probability analysis to conduct advanced pattern recognition. In contrast with first-wave AI, second-wave perceives and learns—sometimes more effectively than humans.

- Yet as Dr. Bhardwaj points out: "These programs still cannot fully replace human assessment because they have not matched humans' capacity for deep data interpretation."

- The Third-Wave AI: This involves emerging programs which can generate novel hypotheses. These technologies are capable of examining huge data sets, identifying statistical patterns and creating algorithms to explain the patterns. Although they still have a long way to go, these systems have enormously exciting futures.

The enormous potential of third-wave AI programs lies in their ability to increase the quantity of data that can be meaningfully analyzed. The programs identify connections between previously unassociated data points by normalizing the contexts of various points to allow simultaneous generation and testing of novel hypotheses in a host of healthcare scenarios. As a result, they can both learn from and explain complex statistical patterns in order to then teach humans what is learned.

IBM's "Watson for Health" is applying cognitive technology to unlock vast amounts of health data. The program can reportedly review and store every medical journal, symptom and case study of treatment and response around the world— doing so exponentially faster than any human.

Google's "DeepMind Health" is working in partnership with clinicians, researchers and patients to solve healthcare problems. The technology is described to combine machine learning and systems neuroscience to build powerful general-purpose learning algorithms into neural networks that mimic the human brain.

Physician and Stanford University Professor Dr. Robert Pearl reports that today's most common AI uses are in algorithmic evidence-based approaches which are programmed by researchers and clinicians. Writing in Forbes.com, he cites key examples:[95]

- Cancer Treatment Protocols: Using consensus algorithms from experts in the field, along with the data that oncologists enter into the medical record (i.e., a patient's age, genetics, cancer staging and associated medical problems), a computer can review dozens, sometimes hundreds, of established treatment alternatives and recommend the most appropriate combination of chemotherapy drugs for a patient.

- Cancer Screening: Computer programs excel at human pattern recognition tasks where the human eye fails even in the best clinicians. Independent studies have found that 50 percent to 63 percent of women who get regular mammograms over 10 years will receive at least one "false-positive" (a test result that is wrong indicates the possibility of cancer, thus requiring additional testing, and sometimes, unnecessary procedures). As many as one-third of the time, two or three radiologists looking at the same mammography will disagree on their interpretation of the results.

- Visual pattern recognition software, which can store tens of thousands of images, is estimated to be 5 to 10 percent more accurate than the average physician.

- Diagnostics: Powerful deep-learning AI applications are advancing in such diagnostic fields as radiology (CT, MRI and mammography diagnoses), pathology (microscopic and cytological diagnoses), dermatology (rash identification and pigmented lesion evaluation for potential melanoma) and ophthalmology (retinal vessel examination to predict the risk for diabetic retinopathy and cardiovascular disease).

- A medical start-up called "Arterys" has a program that can perform a magnetic-resonance imaging analysis of blood flow through a heart in just 15 seconds—this compared with 45 minutes required by humans.

- Surgery: Medical robots can already assist surgeons in removing damaged organs and cancerous tissue. In 2016, a prototype robotic surgeon called Smart Tissue Autonomous Robot (STAR) outperformed human surgeons in a test in which both had to repair the severed intestine of a live pig.

AI-related technologies are finding life-extending and life-saving uses in the general public realm as well. A proliferation of consumer wearables and other medical devices combined with AI are being applied to oversee early-stage heart disease, enabling doctors and other caregivers to better monitor and detect potentially life-threatening episodes at earlier, more treatable stages.

Such advancements offer both the incentives and means to become more deeply involved and interested in our own health, especially when we can easily share these data sets with our health practitioners in a more accurate and structured way. As Dr. Pearl predicts:

> Over time, patients will be able to use a variety of AI tools to care for themselves, just as they manage so many other aspects of their lives today. It may not happen soon...But sometime in the future—more years than entrepreneurs would like and fewer years than most doctors hope—AI will disrupt healthcare

as we know it. Of that we can be sure.

Pearl adds:

> *Unfortunately, the biggest barrier to artificial intelligence in medicine isn't mathematics. Rather, it's a medical culture that values doctor intuition over evidence-based solutions. Physicians cling to their independence and hate being told what to do. Getting them comfortable with the idea of a machine looking over their shoulder as they practice will prove very difficult for years to come.*

On a more hopeful note...for medical professionals, Pearl concludes:

> *Without question, the role of the physician will change in the future. Fortunately for doctors, however, computers have yet to demonstrate the kind of empathy and compassion that millions of patients rely on in their medical care.*

AI Impacts upon the Practice of Law

Any legal profession job that involves lots of mundane document reviews (what lawyers spend a lot of time doing) is also vulnerable to human obsolescence. Software programs such as "e-discovery" are already being used by companies to scan legal papers and predict which documents are relevant.

This can save clients from lots of billable hour charges. Kira Systems, for example, has reportedly cut the time that some lawyers need to review contracts by 20 to 60 percent.

Meanwhile, new user-friendly software applications such as LegalZoom and Rocket Lawyer are providing direct minimum-cost public access alternatives to justice by enabling clients to solve their own problems without consulting legal experts.

In his book *Tomorrow's Lawyers: An Introduction to Your Future*, Oxford University Law Professor Richard Susskind identifies three primary drivers of change that will challenge the future of the market for legal services: the "more-for-less" challenge, liberalization in business structures and information technology. He regards this as perhaps the most misunderstood and under-appreciated catalyst of change in service delivery.[96]

Susskind argues that while many lawyers believe that information technology is overhyped, this perspective misses the larger trend exemplified by the persistence of Moore's law: the astounding growth of accessible digital information.

Echoing much of Susskind's point of view, Mark McKamey believes that AI advancements will inevitably influence law practice due to a complimentary compatibility and fit with human abilities. He emphasizes that computers can be programmed to reason at a high-level relatively easily, but struggle with low-level sensorimotor tasks.[97]

Writing in the *Appeal Law Journal*, McKamey observes that "e-discovery" software can already sift through enormous sets of documents to help determine their potential relevance to a special case...during the processes of discovery, for example.

Citing a study by Maura Grossman and Gordon Cormack, McKamey notes:

> [T]echnology-assisted review can (and does) yield
> more accurate results than exhaustive manual review,
> with much lower effort.

The Author says that other articles further emphasize the cost benefits of e-discovery, which can amount to savings of 70 percent or more.

Emerging AI systems can also offer legal opinions...for example, advice to a client regarding what the value of a particular personal injury claim might be.

None of this suggests that human judgment will become irrelevant. While lawyers and paralegal assistants will spend far less time sifting through documents, they will continue to remain indispensable to the process.

Mark McKamey points out that law is messy, making it difficult to construct algorithms that capture the law in a useful way. Few legal problems have clear yes or no answers. Legal reasoning is inherently a "parallel process" in which the answer to one question may change which questions are subsequently asked...a problem that can significantly disrupt the ability of computers to deliver useful answers to legal questions.

Citing Evgeny Morosov's book *To Save Everyrthing, Click Here: Technology, Utopianism, and the Urge to Fix Problems that Don't Exist*, McKamey warns about a worrisome "solutionism" trend that results from excessive computer dependence:

> *Solutionism is a kind of technological determinism...the technological solutions available for minor problems...lead us to shallow thinking, and our goals divert from understanding large, complex social problems into writing yet more apps. Worse, we start seeing only problems that can be solved by apps as problems worth solving.*

McKamey is particularly concerned that solutionism can creep into new legal technology applications with a commercial focus that obscures justice as the ultimate goal of the legal system.

At the same time, new user-friendly applications are also increasing public access to justice by enabling clients to solve their own problems without consulting legal experts. A boom of legal outside disruption innovation companies is already underway. LegalZoom and Rocket Lawyer, which began by servicing the low-margin end of the market, are ramping their way up and now competing with traditional firms that had abandoned those markets.

111

Outside pressure from non-traditional legal service providers now leaves traditional practitioners little choice but to embrace technological change more fully. As Richard Susskind submits:

> *[It] is simply inconceivable that information technology will radically alter all corners of our economy and society and yet somehow legal work will be exempt from any change.*

AI Impacts upon Banking and Financial Markets

The McKinsey & Company researchers estimate a potential to additionally automate up to 43 percent of all financial and insurance services. Mortgage brokers, for example, spend as much as 90 percent of their time processing applications.

More sophisticated verification processes for documents and credit applications could reduce that proportion to about 60 percent.

Big banks are now using software programs that can suggest financial market bets, construct hedges and act as robo-economists, using natural language. BlackRock, the biggest fund company in the world, has replaced some highly-paid pickers with computer algorithms.

Hedge funds are already using AI to beat the stock market, Google is using it to diagnose heart disease more quickly and accurately and American Express is deploying bots to serve its customers online.

Jim Marcus, co-publisher of *The Financial Brand* and publisher of the *Digital Banking Report*, says that the explosive growth of structured and unstructured data, availability of new technologies such as cloud computing and machine learning algorithms, rising pressures brought by new competition, increased regulation and heightened consumer expectations have created a "perfect storm" for the expanded use of artificial intelligence in financial services. He writes:

> *The benefits of AI in banks and credit unions are widespread, reaching back office operations, compliance, customer experience, product delivery, risk management and marketing to name a few. Suddenly, banking organizations can work with large histories of data for every decision made.*[98]

Although as of yet most banks and credit unions are in the early stages of adopting AI technologies, an estimated 32 percent of financial services executives surveyed have confirmed using AI technologies such as predictive analytics, recommendation engines and voice recognition and response.

A large benefit is that AI makes it possible to automate vast amounts of data, analyzing and applying it at record speeds. In addition, new cognitive-based solutions enable a more proactive and personal customer experience at a lower cost than was ever possible before. This is driven by AI's ability to build knowledge at high speed, understand natural language and run operational processes in a fully compliant fashion.

Marcus reports that despite some early hesitation in the industry around the commitment to AI, there are several use cases. The number one trend identified in 2017 *Retail Banking Trends and Predictions* was that customers are willing to share their personal information if they can receive custom advice, offers and service based on this shared insight. These personalized communications and advice capabilities are enabled by robo-advisors—online wealth management services that provide automated, algorithm-based portfolio management advice without the help of a human counterpart.

AI algorithms can regularly rebalance the portfolios to maintain the original investment guidelines and operate at costs less than 100 basis points (compared to 2-3 percent for traditional brokers). Initially promoted by fintech firms like Betterment and Wealthfront, robo-advisors are now part of the offerings at traditional brokers as well.

The banking and financial services industry is taking advantage of AI to perform routine, repetitive processes more efficient and effective. A once very tedious process of new "customer onboarding communication," for example, can now become highly personalized interactions based on an individual's previous banking activities. This level of personalization was almost impossible to achieve without the benefits of machine learning and AI.

Another AI application is to continuously update compliance requirements, customer informational documentation and even product "frequently asked question" responses. With a foundation of continuously changing facts and product updates, all related communications can be changed immediately.

Marcus observes that AI is becoming vital to prevent, monitor, detect and respond to potential and actual fraud attempts in real-time.

He predicts that with an origin rooted in risk and fraud detection and cost reduction, AI will be increasingly important to enable financial services firms to be competitive:

> This is just the tip of the iceberg. Soon, all financial services firms will leverage the power of AI to deliver better experiences, lower costs, reduce risks and increase revenues.

AI Impacts upon Manufacturing

Matthew Randall, the executive director of York College's Center for Professional Excellence, writes in TechCrunch.com that the trend of industrial robots replacing human manufacturing jobs is ultimately a good thing:

In the last century, we moved from people manually building cars to robots assembling cars. As a result, manufacturers both produce more cars and employ more people per car than before. Instead of performing dangerous tasks, those workers now program the robots to do the dirty work for them—and get paid more for doing so. As long as we've had technology, we've had Luddites who literally destroy technological advancements—and yet, here we are, more productive, with higher quality of living than ever.

Randall argues:

[In] reality, [robots] will enable us to keep more (and better) jobs at home, to grow our local industry, to improve our lives at the micro and macro levels. With greater automation, efficiency, safety and productivity, the North American manufacturing sector will not only survive, it will showcase the power of our innovation and ingenuity.

He concludes:

So, will a robot take your job? Maybe, but in return, you—and your children and grandchildren—will likely find more meaningful work, for better pay. Sounds like a good trade-off to me.[99]

The emergence of an AI revolution in what is chronicled as a "second machine age" is exemplified by rapid advancements and influences of industrial 3-D printing technologies. No longer limited to preliminary equipment prototyping and rapid tooling, it is now serving endlessly diverse manufacturing applications, including the creation of entire jet engines, medical and dental devices, lenses for light-emitting diodes (LEDs) and home appliance parts to name a tiny sampling.

More and more companies are joining the revolution as the range of printable materials continues to expand. In addition to basic plastics and photosensitive resins, they already include ceramics, cement, glass, numerous metals and new thermoplastic composites infused with carbon nanotubes and fibers.

The technology fabricates an object layer-by-layer according to a digital "blueprint" downloaded to a printer which allows not only for limitless customization, but also for designs of great intricacy.

That being said, traditional injection-molding presses can spit out thousands of widgets an hour. Three-D processes are slower but catching up. While still slower, since each unit is built independently, they can easily be modified to meet unique needs.

Writing in the *Harvard Business Review*, Richard D'Aveni notes that a big 3-D printing advantage is that pieces that used to be molded separately and then assembled can be produced as one piece in a single run. D'Aveni cites a simple example of sunglasses:

> *The 3-D process allows the porosity and mixture of plastics to vary in different areas of the frame. The earpieces come out soft and flexible, while the rims holding the lenses are hard. No assembly required.*[100]

Richard D'Aveni further explains that printing parts and products also allows them to be designed with more complex architectures, such as honeycombing within steel panels or geometries previously too fine to mill. Complex mechanical parts—an encased set of gears, for example—can be made without assembly.

D'Aveni explains:

Additive methods can be used to combine parts and generate far more interior detailing in products...such as jet engines. GE Aviation uses the technology to create a nozzle that used to be assembled from 20 separately cast parts. Now, it's fabricated in one piece in order to cut costs of manufacturing by 75 percent.

What's more, 3-D printing applications are tackling complex large-scale construction challenges which have previously involved a variety of highly specialized technology operations. So-called "big area additive manufacturing" makes it possible to create endo- and exoskeletons of entire jet fighters, including the body, wings, internal structural panels, embedded wiring and antennas and soon, the entire central load-bearing structure. This makes use of a huge gantry with computerized controls to move the printers into position.

To borrow from an old aphorism...the sky is no limit for 3-D printing.

Yes, 3-D printing and other revolutionary advances will transform the ways we live and in ways we can't presently even imagine just as major technological evolutions always do. Previous generations before modern farm equipment came along couldn't have foreseen that it would later require 30 times less people to cultivate 100 acres than it does today.

Lots of farm workers lost their jobs in exchange for an ability to produce more crops and livestock necessary to feed growing populations at affordable prices.

And while the Model T turned out the lights on many professions including blacksmiths and carriage makers, its introduction of affordable automobiles through mass production created huge new demands for labor created by the steel, glass, rubber, textile trade and oil and gas industries.

Dystopian visions of massive AI-driven job losses are also premature. Throughout history, employment adapted as machines gradually replaced more and more aspects of labor. While once again, this fourth revolution will eliminate some jobs, it will also create opportunities for new ones that will require and enable more people to think smarter.

Human progress demonstrates that we are a very adaptable lot. After all, we not only survived first Industrial Revolution, but came out of it living better and longer than all preceding generations. This new Information Revolution is already expanding these benefits, while dramatically advancing human mental and physical capacities in the process.

There is no reason to believe that artificial intelligence will replace the need for creative thinking, problem-solving, leadership, teamwork and personal initiative. Far more likely, we humans can leverage technology to provide a smarter and better world.

This book began with no doomsday preconceptions regarding AI, nor does it conclude with one. In any case, it is a natural tendency to impose bias that assumes that tomorrow will resemble our positive and negative experiences today, only a little bit different—or maybe extremely so—instead of recognizing that we are in the middle of an unknowably disruptive change.

While we should expect that there will always be a demand for adaptable and versatile human labor, workers everywhere will indeed need to rethink traditional notions of where they work, how they work and what talents and capabilities they bring to that work.

All of this will require fundamentally resetting our collective intuition regarding how we...humanity, can reinvent versions of ourselves that fit that better world we hope for our children...and for future generations beyond theirs, ad infinitum.

DISRUPTIVE SOCIALIST SEDUCTIONS AND SUCCESSIONS

THERE IS NO turning back the clock or holding back the advances on the myriad of ways that information technology—AI and Internet connectivity in particular—are changing not only our lifestyles, but our fundamental perceptions regarding the social structures we deem most desirable as well.

Enthusiastic proponents promise tantalizingly optimistic visions, including: free money provided by government Universal Basic Income stipends that enable us to pursue more creative and satisfying activities; daily new conveniences previously conceivable in the fertile imaginations of a fiction writer but decades, or even a few years or days, ago; enhanced mobility through shared on-demand transportation services that banish most private automobiles to rusty scrap heaps of oblivion; safety from predatory behaviors of others through ubiquitous, ever-watchful interconnected security devices.

Some of those same technologies afford opportunities for many of us to live and work pretty much wherever and whenever we prefer through digital telecommuting that connects us to clients and employers in an inherently space-less world of increasingly faceless virtual relationships. In all cases, we remain connected and dependent upon ever watchful and tirelessly obedient digital assistants, who, in turn, monitor, record and market private information we generously, often unwittingly, share.

So, on balance, how can each of us assess the ultimate cost-benefit tradeoffs between too-good-to-be-true conveniences and economies and the inevitable socialist-style encroachments upon privacy, autonomy and independence?

In what ways are these accelerating developments transforming personal, business and societal cultures? Should we be compliant and adaptive, and even positively hopeful—or rather...well actually, regarding the latter—there really is no constructive "rather."

Just as with every other major evolutionary game changer—and this is clearly a formatively consequential one—let's get used to the idea and make the most of it.

A Basic Universally Terrible Free Income Idea

Kai-Fu Lee, chairman and CEO of Sinovation Ventures and former president of Google China, observes that a grim vision of AI's disruptive workplace impacts upon concepts of self-worth and what it means to be human has sent many Silicon Valley techno-elites casting urgently about for quick-fix solutions. He told the *Wall Street Journal*:

> As the architects and profiteers of the AI age, they feel
> a mix of genuine social responsibility and fear of
> being targeted when the pitchforks come out.[101]

Lee recognizes the superficial appeal afforded by Universal Basic Income as exactly what Silicon Valley entrepreneurs love: an elegant technical solution to tangled social problems:

> UBI can be the magic wand that lets them wish away
> messy complexities of human psychology and get back

to building technologies that 'make the world a better place,' while making them rich.

Even better, government(s) will provide unconditional cash stipends to pay for all of this. This approach maps well with how the tech establishment tends to view society: as a collection of "users" rather than as citizens, customers and human beings.

Although Lee argues against "simply falling back on an economic painkiller like a universal basic income," he instead proposes a so-called "Social Investment Stipend," a guaranteed salary for those deemed eligible by all-knowing government employment prognosticators. These stipends would fall under three employment eligibility categories: care work, community service and education.

Lee explains that these ordained activities would form the pillars of a "new social contract" that will reward "beneficial activities just as we now reward economically productive activities."

In other words, government employees would be paid by taxpayers to compete with private professionals and service providers in those high-demand fields which are likely to be most resistant to AI disruptions.

As Lee, himself, notes:

> *The jobs that will remain relatively insulated from AI fall on opposite ends of the income spectrum. CEOs, home care nurses and hair stylists are all in 'safe' professions, but the people in some of these professions will be swimming in the riches of the AI revolution while others compete against a vast pool of desperate fellow workers.*

What could possibly go wrong with that?

Quite a lot actually.

Even Lee recognizes that many difficult questions remain to

be answered before we could even consider implementing such a sweeping and idealistic policy. A key unknown he cites is assessing and balancing the urgency to create with the ability to pay for his plan, factors that will depend upon the pace and nature of AI's economic impact.

Ironically, Kai-Fu Lee now appears pessimistic and critical of the very capitalistic free enterprise opportunities that have enabled his own successful entrepreneurial AI business ventures. Viewing the future, he writes:

> *Even where AI doesn't destroy jobs outright, however, it will exacerbate inequality. AI is inherently monopolistic: A company with more data and better algorithms will gain ever more users and data. This self-reinforcing cycle will lead to winner-take-all markets, with one company making massive profits while its rivals languish.*

Lee predicts that many of the free market's self-correcting mechanisms will break down in an AI economy, potentially bringing about "a new caste system, split into a plutocratic AI elite and the powerless struggling masses." He foresees that since most of us tie our personal worth to the pursuit of work and success:

> *In the coming years, people will watch algorithms and robots easily outmaneuver them at tasks they've spent a lifetime mastering. I fear that this will lead to a crushing feeling of futility and obsolescence. At worst, it will lead people to question their own worth and what it means to be human.*

Several major Silicon Valley entrepreneurs who are developing the very technologies that fuel fears of a dystopian future—and often profiting handsomely from them—are endorsing UBI as a potential fix.

Proponents claim that UBI will insulate displaced workers from poverty and quell the potential for unrest during a profound and painful economic transition. Some argue that it also might spur innovation by encouraging more people to take entrepreneurial risks.

Facebook founder Mark Zuckerberg has made this latter case for UBI. Speaking to Harvard's graduating class in May 2017, he said:

> *We should have a society that measures progress not just by economic metrics like GDP, but by how many of us have a role we find meaningful.*
> [...]
> *We should explore ideas like universal basic income, to make sure that everyone has a cushion to try new ideas.*[102]

Others are not so sanguine about UBI costs and consequences for a variety of reasons. They argue that UBI will undermine productivity by rewarding laziness; that it is simply socialism by another name and violates core tenets of capitalism; and that it is based upon a false assumption that this technological revolution won't create better jobs tomorrow to replace the ones it erases today.

And, oh yes...UBI will bankrupt the U.S. economy and transfer hopeless debts to future generations.

Silicon Valley investor Sam Altman, CEO of Y Combinator, has launched a pilot test program to see what a UBI future might look like. His company's research arm plans to pay up to 100 recipient households between $12,000 to $18,000 in exchange for...nothing.[103]

Although the free money recipients are asked to submit to occasional surveys, there are no preconditions nor penalties for failing to do so. The idea is to give people money without preconditions and observe what they choose to do.

Altman, who is branded as a new-company coach whose firm helped launch stars like Airbnb, Zenefits, and Dropbox, hopes that other high-tech companies will expand his initiative into a much larger study involving thousands of households in multiple states. The idea is to demonstrate within a few years that UBI can bring about long-term positive impacts.

Quoting Marco Annunziata, former Chief Economist and Head of Business Innovation Strategy at General Electric:

> Like a zombie, [UBI] keeps coming back. Like zombie movies, it enjoys growing popularity by defying logic and common sense.[104]

Noting that if you ask, "why do we need UBI?," Annunziata says that most proponents respond "because the robots will soon take our jobs." They are also likely to assert that countless Silicon Valley start-up wizards including Elon Musk and Mark Zuckerberg favor the idea and that UBI is already being tested in many places.

Annunziata warns that the fact that UBI appeals most to cities which have already gone bankrupt or have financial prospects of doing so should give us pause. He offers recent UBI proposals in Chicago and Stockton, California, as prime examples.

Referring to UBI as a "universally bad idea," Annunziata's 2019 *Forbes* article opines:

> Facebook co-founder Chris Hughes' Economic Security Project contributed $1 million to nearly fully fund Stockton's one-year UBI experiment. That's headline-grabbing charity. If you truly believe there will be no more jobs, you should set up a perpetual endowment to help fund UBI. If you think people need help finding their career path, you could give them jobs or

education and training opportunities.

If you ask enthusiasts, "why are they testing UBI," the likely answer is "To make sure people will use it to learn new skills and look for a job, or set up their own business."

Following this train of logic, Annunziata suggests that when you think about this, then wonder:

> *In other words, we run pilot projects to make sure UBI will not stop people from looking for a job. But...you just told me there will be no jobs...*

Annunziata adds:

> *The reason people run UBI experiments, of course, is they do not believe for a second that the machines will do all the work. Which means that to finance UBI, enough people will have to work, produce, earn and be taxed. Hence the concern on how UBI would impact work incentives.*

Regarding those more thoughtful proponents that say we need UBI so that everyone can be freed to pursue their passions, Annunziata believes that this utopian notion clashes with two unpleasant truths:

> *First: since we need human work to improve our lot, the priority is to make sure everyone contributes to the best of their abilities;*

> *Second: these abilities are very unequally distributed. Not everyone has a passion, and not everyone is equally talented. This is a simple fact of life.*

Annunziata points out that not everyone can be either an artist nor an entrepreneur:

> *Our economies need construction workers, welders, plumbers, electricians, nurses, firemen, policemen, janitors, waiters. Some people go into some of these jobs with passion, others because it pays the bills— and these jobs need to be done.*

Nevertheless, Annunziata believes that Silicon Valley can and should help foster learning, skilling and reskilling, both with funding and by developing new technologies. Those working in this direction are part of the solution; those grandstanding on UBI are part of the problem.

The devilishly hard challenge, Annunziata believes, is to strike the right balance between providing assistance and incentives; to combine strong incentives to work with the assurance that if you lose your job you are still likely to be okay.

> *[Here] UBI would send exactly that wrong-headed message, reducing people's incentive to work. And it would get worse. Our concept of a dignified life is relative. Getting by on my guaranteed basic income, I will look at my richer, working peers and feel that my lifestyle is not quite dignified.*
>
> *So I will lobby politicians for an increase in UBI. As UBI rises, even fewer people will work; those who still work will have to be taxed more, and so even fewer people will work, and...*

In the end, Annunziata argues, UBI is like granting open-ended unemployment benefits with no requirement to look for work or financing an indefinite 'gap year' to anyone who wants it. Even if it was a nice thing to do, we just don't have the money.

Andrew Ng, a former chief scientist at the Chinese Internet company Baidu, co-founder of Google's deep learning research team and also co-founder of Coursera, an online education company, favors a UBI variation he calls "Conditional Basic Income."[105]

Speaking at the 2018 *Wall Street Journal* "The Future of Everything Festival," Mr. Ng said:

> For someone that's unemployed I really support the government giving a safety net with the expectation that they'll do something to contribute back so they can gain the skills to re-enter the workforce.

Ng agrees that while AI companies will continue to bring in massive amounts of value, there is a need to correct public misconceptions regarding what their technologies actually can and cannot accomplish. He recalls:

> This has happened to me multiple times, where I would listen to a CEO on stage make an announcement about what their company is doing with AI, and then 20 minutes later I'd talk with one of their engineers, and they'd say, 'No, we're not doing that, and we have no idea how to do it.'...it's possible for companies to make promises very publicly that are just not feasible.

Former Mitt Romney domestic policy advisor and National Review contributor Oren Cass is far more optimistic about the AI future. He agrees that the real work issue regarding whether and how people are employed as contributors to society's productive system "is both an economic and cultural question." However, UBI and other proposals for government handout solutions aren't the answer.[106]

Interviewed by Jason Willick in the *Wall Street Journal*, Cass believes that "the further down the income ladder you go, generally speaking, the less enthusiasm there is for redistribution as a solution. People will tell you they want to work."

Cass rejects fat cat Silicon Valley solutions where many of those who get to the top of income distribution hierarchies suggest "Why can't I just write a check?"

The reason, as Cass points out, is that Karl Marx was wrong in speculating that workers with leisure time would "hunt in the morning, fish in the afternoon, rear cattle in the evening, criticize after dinner." People on disability insurance—specially men—are more likely to be "sleeping and watching TV than hunting or fishing," Mr. Cass says.

Oren Cass notes that Hillary Clinton's 2016 campaign workshopped a version of the UBI, and Sen. Kamala Harris has proposed an expansion of the earned-income tax credit that would have a similar effect.

He adds that people want to "know what our obligations are, and feel that we're fulfilling them."

When the foundation of the social work ethic starts to crumble, political upheaval tends to follow. But no, this won't result because all the jobs are becoming automated. As Cass foresees the future:

> In almost all cases, technology is a complement to work, not a substitute—in fact, it increases workers' value.

Telecommuting on the Internet Superhighway

From a highly individualistically liberating perspective, telecommuting to work through communication links rather than through physical presence now enables a new breed of entrepreneurs and employees to conduct business in sweatpants and shorts from geographically-dispersed satellite offices, personal homes and vacation retreats. This growing trend represents a substantial departure from a traditional urban model where employment is predominately concentrated in a population center such as a major city's Central Business District (CBD).

According to a 2017 Gallup survey, more Americans are not only working remotely, but they are also doing so for longer periods. Forty-three percent of the more than 15,000 adults surveyed said that they spent at least some time doing so, a four percent increase since a previous 2012 poll.

The share who said they spent a day or less a week working remotely shrank substantially from 2012 to 2016, falling to 25 percent from 34 percent. At the same time, the share that reported working remotely four to five days a week grew by nearly the same amount, rising to 31 percent from 24 percent.[107]

Many employees and employers have recognized important benefits which continue to encourage remote work and associated flexible scheduling practices. Gallup found that such opportunities often played a major role in an employee's decision to take or leave a job. The report said:

> *Employees are pushing companies to break down the long-established structures and policies that traditionally have influenced their workdays.*

Although widespread and on the rise across all industries, some types of businesses and organizations reported better successes with remote working arrangements than others. The concept was particularly popular in finance, insurance, real estate, transportation, manufacturing, construction and retail industries where those who reported working remotely rose eight percentage points to 47 percent from 2012 to 2016. There were also steady gains in healthcare, law and public policy.

Well over half of all employees in transportation, computer, information systems and mathematics fields worked remotely some of the time. However, remote work had become less common than in 2012 for Americans employed in the fields of community and social services; science, engineering and architecture; and education, training and libraries.

While both employees and some employers viewed remote work arrangements to be broadly beneficial, even those representing popular industry applications reported struggling with the extent it should be embraced. For example, Yahoo and the insurance giant Aetna, which had originally pioneered such plans, had second thoughts regarding negative influences upon collaborative engagement.

Perhaps surprisingly, in 2012 the workers who said they felt most engaged with the employing organization while working remotely were those who spent the least amount of time off-site. By 2016, that was no longer true...those who spent none or all of their time out of the office reported feeling equally engaged. In fact, those who spent 60 percent to 80 percent of their time away from the office expressed the highest rates of engagement. Gallup reported:

> In spite of the additional time away from managers and co-workers, they are the most likely of all employees to strongly agree that someone at work cares about them as a person, encourages their development and has talked to them about their progress.

It is natural to expect remote working arrangements to cause employing business cultures to become far more impersonal as places where people don't really get to know each other: who, for example, is having a personal problem or celebrating a birthday? Employees don't meet the boss in the elevator. They don't discuss casual ideas that give rise to important opportunities. They don't share corporate or individual achievements. They become environments where "every man (and woman) is an island."

Counterintuitively, Gallup reported that those who spent

three or four days a week working remotely were also the most likely to report thinking that they had a best friend at work and had opportunities for professional growth.

Writing in the Harvard Business Review, Sean Graber posits "why remote work thrives in some companies and fails in others." He explains:

> *Successful remote work is based on three core principles: communication, coordination, and culture. Broadly speaking, communication is the ability to exchange information, coordination is the ability to work around a common goal, and culture is a shared set of customs that foster trust and engagement.*[108]

Graber points out that a special challenge to success is that communication in a virtual environment can make it more difficult to explain complex ideas. This results when a lack of face-to-face interaction limits social cues, which may often lead to misunderstandings and potential conflicts. This can be particularly true when people aren't able to ask questions and carry on discussions in real time.

Sean Graber also warns that failures of opportunities to meet face-to-face can also degrade and compromise a company's social and working culture. This can occur, for example, when out-of-office individuals become inclined to focus on their individual task assignments at the expense of team spirit and collaboration.

Here again, information technology is reconnecting and extending virtual face-to-face teleconferencing opportunities across boundless business, professional and social landscapes. Even small offices and organizations with no offices at all now have access to high-speed Internet and cheap web cameras, headsets, speakers and even smartphones.

Video teleconferencing is becoming enormously popular for a variety of reasons. It affords a means to host meetings from locations anywhere: to visually and verbally communicate with dispersed audiences in real-time; to discuss and resolve time-critical matters; to share, exchange, create and approve documents; to record, save and re-distribute proceedings in text and video formats; and to accomplish all of this on short notice and without incurring travel and lodging expenses.

Organizations ranging from large corporations to small start-ups can also mutually enjoy substantial benefits afforded through remote tele-employment. Key among these, the strategy enables them to recruit and retain the best people no matter where they live, to buy a unit of service and labor at lower salary and overhead prices and to minimize personnel facility requirements.

Forbes contributor William Arruda believes that the biggest winners in flexible work programs are the company employees. Notwithstanding the fact that the Internet connects businesses to specialized freelance solopreneurs who compete for their work projects and jobs, business operations in general will increasingly decentralize.

Arruda writes:

> [T]he new trend that's exciting me and is growing exponentially is the area of remote work that's not for freelancers; it's for employees. There's no arguing that the 9-to-5, 40-hour work week, with your entire team located near you, is gone. And it's not coming back. Today, it is more likely that you work on a team where some or even all of your colleagues work remotely.[109]

Also writing in Forbes.com, Tiffany Williams enthusiastically foresees enormous business networking and service market opportunities for new generations of work-from-home "digital nomads" who are now enabled to strike individually self-determined balances between their personal and professional lives. Practitioners working from mobile virtual offices have become free to travel, spend more quality time with families and friends, pursue educational goals and special hobbies and attend to medical issues.[110]

Internet connectivity now instantly hooks up anyone with a laptop or smartphone to markets and products throughout the world. Anything from accounting, legal transcription, writing and marketing can be accomplished remotely. Advanced information processing software, which was previously used only by corporate enterprises due to lack of affordability, can now be accessed through the cloud.

Williams observes the rapidly growing popularity of commission-based product and service marketing businesses strategies, which are ideal for home businesses. Online networking enables businesses to concentrate only on producing and delivering great products and services and outsource promotion to outside professionals who are compensated according to sales performance.

Home-connected businesses afford working parents and students flexibility to arrange schedules around other priorities. Living close to their children's schools and avoiding long work commutes enables more time to spend with them and less money to spend on day care costs. Online teaching and training programs enable home-based business parents and others to advance learning goals such as attainment of additional knowledge-based skills and credentials.

Andrea Loubier emphasizes that telecommuting benefits, whether through arrangements with primary employers or solo entrepreneurship from homes or close-by neighborhood offices, are about much more than just enabling happy campers to conduct business from Starbucks or beach blankets. Writing in Forbes.com, she observes:

> It allows workers to retain more of their time in the
> day and adjust to their personal mental and physical

> *well-being needs that optimize productivity.*
> *Removing something as simple as a twenty-minute*
> *commute to work can make all world of difference. If*
> *you are ill, telecommuting allows one to recover faster*
> *without being forced to be in the office.* [111]

Loubier is enthusiastic about benefits to corporate business employers as well. For example, it can increase employee performance and productivity by reducing distractions such as water cooler gossip. Telecommuting arrangements can also dramatically reduce business operating costs. She writes:

> *According to Aetna, an insurance giant in America, it*
> *shed 2.7 million square feet of office space and as a*
> *result saved $78 million. American Express reported*
> *similar results by saving $10-15 million annually*
> *thanks to its telecommuting policies.*

Telecommuters can save big on cost of living benefits as well. No longer required to locate near a teeming metropolis, home buyers can escape having to pay exorbitant housing prices to live in densely-packed cities and near-by high-priced suburbs. Telecommuters are no longer required to endure daily hours on congested traffic lanes which could be spent in more satisfying and productive pursuits.

Telecommuters can select home sites that offer special cultural, economic, educational and natural amenities which are most important to them and their families: locations which are safest and which offer the best schools for their children; places near other loved ones, including aging parents; settings with access to convenient retail services, and where they can enjoy treasured outdoor landscapes and activities; and communities where people make it a point to know neighbors and to engage long-term friendships.

Exercising Urban Fight or Flight Reflexes

So, what influences and impacts will rapid advancements and expanding applications of smart technology have upon these economic, social and political divides? As predicated upon rationale that follows, I foresee that they will become increasingly contentious.

First, the Internet now affords greater opportunity for people to freely choose where they live. More and more who work for large metropolitan-based corporations will telecommute rather than physically travel on highways or public transportation. This will benefit companies by reducing their need to provide costly urban working facilities. They'll be able to expand their talent pool on the basis of need, without regard to geographic considerations.

Second, many of those Internet-connected corporate service providers, along with other independent entrepreneurial businesses both large and small, can reside wherever their lifestyle choices lead them. Those decisions will take a variety of considerations into account, very much including location-based cost of living values, family-based community assessments, access to preferred natural and cultural settings, ties to familiar and cherished social structures and of course, availability of essential revenue opportunities.

Third, and as previously discussed, AI and automation will disproportionately impact some work and employment markets both to the benefit and detriment of others. While we can expect cities, suburbs and rural areas to win some and lose some competitive advantages, each of us are likely to bring our personal life experiences and biases into any speculations regarding true winners and losers. Here, I plead no exception.

Fourth, let's perhaps assume, as a general rule, that many work and employment opportunities that have traditionally involved metropolitan-based specialized expertise, law and medicine, for example, are displaced by AI servants, and that simultaneously, large metropolitan-centered hospitals, for example, are supplanted by smaller, more broadly distributed AI-supported community clinics—at suburban and rural locations with greater abundance of affordable personal healthcare workers.

Finally, in the large scheme of things, let's imagine very different demographically-influenced responses to various government policy proposals premised upon remediating "income-inequality" impacts of labor-intensive job losses to automation. Some highly industrial cities, along with suburban and rural communities, particularly those in less prosperous locales, will have greater stakes than others.

Broadly viewed, it's popularly accepted that cities, suburbs and the rural countryside all offer different living experiences which various people prefer. For example, a city dweller is likely to place a higher value on easier access to more business, entertainment and museum/theater culture than someone who lives in a rural area. The rural countryside lifestyle is far cheaper than living in a city, and some may find themselves driving hours to get to a movie theater or a grocery store.

Which technological solutions "the world" is willing to accept will continue to depend a lot upon individual world perspectives viewed from diverse and divergent geographical, social, economic, ideological and lifestyle-oriented vantage points.

Some will more readily accept the China model, premised upon wholesale trades of personal privacy in exchange for "higher" social benefits afforded by public security, improved energy and infrastructure efficiencies and special privilege incentives awarded to individuals based upon government-dictated and monitored good behavior merits. This model might portend rather grim "smart cities" trending.

Others will be less likely to embrace wired-together metropolitan convenience vs. losses of privacy. Individual autonomy tradeoffs may increasingly opt for more suburban and rural lifestyles afforded by Internet-connected remote entrepreneurship and telecommuting opportunities. This trend, in combination with the former, will likely deepen ideological and political demographics nationwide, and regional and local divides.

A 2017 *Washington Post Family Foundation* opinion poll revealed substantial lifestyle priority and political differences between Americans living in rural settings versus metropolitan centers. A key finding was that this divide is more cultural than economic in nature, and these convictions were held most strongly in rural communities.[112]

The survey of nearly 1,700 Americans—including more than 1,000 adults living in rural areas and small towns—found a deep-seated kinship in rural America, coupled with a stark sense of estrangement from people who live in urban areas. Nearly 7 in 10 rural residents said that their values differed from those of people who live in big cities, including 4 in 10 who said that their values are "very different." By comparison, about half of the urban residents say their values differ from rural people, with less than 20 percent of urbanites believing that rural values are "very different."

Rural misgivings regarding metropolitan attitudes included predominate concerns about America's rapidly changing demographics, a sense that traditional Christian values are under siege and a perception that the federal government primarily caters most to the needs of people in big cities.

The survey showed that key differences between rural and urban America ultimately center on fairness, with questions regarding:

> *Who wins and loses in the new American economy, who deserves the most help in society and whether the federal government shows preferential treatment to certain types of people.*

When asked which is more common—that government help tends to go to irresponsible people who do not deserve it or that it doesn't reach people in need—rural Americans are more likely than others to say they think people are abusing the system.

Rural Americans were also broadly skeptical that the federal government is fair or effective at improving people's economic situations. More than 60 percent said that federal efforts to improve living standards either make things worse or have little impact. Those views appear to feed the rural-urban divide: A 56 percent majority of rural residents says the federal government does more to help people living in and around large cities, while 37 percent feel they treat both urban and rural areas equally.

Rural and metropolitan survey respondents both expressed widespread concerns about the lack of jobs in communities. Two-thirds of rural residents rated local job opportunities as fair or poor, compared with about half of urban residents. Nearly 6 of 10 rural residents said that they would encourage young people in their community to leave for more opportunity elsewhere.

According to Census Bureau data, the poverty rates are similar, 16 percent in cities and 17 percent in rural areas. However, as discussed later, these statistics, based entirely on "money income," fail to account for a variety of value-laden government benefit transfers to low-income recipients and are very misleading. Taken altogether, it is difficult to quantify the extent to which these de facto federal government poverty subsidies work to the special advantage of either demographic set addressed in the poll.[113]

The *Washington Post Family Foundation* opinion poll results highlighted deepening conservative versus liberal political divisions between rural and urban Americans. While urban counties favored Hillary Clinton by 32 percentage points in the 2016 election, rural and small-town voters backed Trump by a

26-point margin, significantly wider than GOP nominee Mitt Romney's 16 points four years earlier.

Most rural residents polled said that they believed that key elements of President Trump's economic agenda would help their local economy. Large majorities attributed this optimism to infrastructure investments, better foreign trade deals, a crackdown on undocumented immigrant workers, lower business taxes and government deregulation.

The survey responses, along with follow-up interviews and focus groups the pollsters conducted in rural Ohio, brought into view a portrait of a split that is tied even more to social identity than to economic experience.

A vast majority of rural Americans judged their communities favorably as places where people look out for each other, which was cited as a point of pride and distinction they say they can't find in urban centers. One follow-up survey responder, Ryan Lawson, who grew up in northern Wisconsin, was quoted as saying:

> *Being from a rural area, everyone looks out for each other. People in my experience, in cities are not as compassionate toward their neighbor as people in rural parts.*

Lifestyle Matters

So okay, technology-enabled remote work opportunities are likely to attract more and more people to rural and "small town" community lifestyles. Nevertheless, lots of people prefer living in them too, and there is every reason to believe that many more will continue to do so.

Some common portrayals of demographic differences, including those with political roots and overtones, become exaggerated, stereotypic and even humorous. As Americans, just as citizens of other nations, we share a common history, common cultural and family values, common economic needs and self-fulfillment aspirations and a common future. We celebrate our independence to speak and live freely, and we celebrate our enrichment and empowerment afforded by non-prejudicial diversity.

To a substantial degree, we Americans exercise our wonderful freedoms through residency lifestyle preferences relative to income requirements. Consider, for example, that the average 2017 monthly rental cost for a two-bedroom Manhattan apartment was $3,422, although admittedly this is an extreme case.[114]

Smaller cities typically offer much cheaper rental prices, property costs and real estate taxes in widely differing ranges. Even in New York City, rent in the East Village is far pricier than in the South Bronx.

Overall, the average monthly rent in U.S. cities and suburbs was $1,640, with suburbs averaging $1,695—just $50 more expensive. Although luxury homes in the country can also be very expensive, typical rural housing prices are much more affordable than those in urban or suburban communities.

Whereas large cities consist of many thousands or millions of people living in close proximity and set a costly premium on personal space, suburban settings offer a balance; three and-four-bedroom houses are common, as are houses with multiple stories, basements and garages. Nevertheless, many young and older people everywhere will continue to be content with life in small studio apartments with a roommate or as single-person lifestyles.

Families more typically prefer a home with a reasonable amount of outdoor space for kids and pets. Rural living expands affordable yard space, affords more privacy and extends more immediate access to the natural landscape, family and individual outdoor recreation activities.

Transportation requirements, options and economies will continue to be different in urban, suburban and rural communities over the foreseeable future. Some circumstances will continue to depend heavily upon riding trains, subways and buses.

Suburban areas, depending upon size and proximity to metropolitan population centers, will continue to represent various mixes of private vehicle and public transportation connections. Small towns, and rural areas most particularly, will continue to rely predominantly upon private vehicles.

So, in balance, while rural and suburban dwellers may spend less on housing, many—depending again on specific location—may wind up spending more on transportation. On the other hand, country living frees residents from having to worry about buying public transportation passes, scheduling activities around transportation and the hassles of transferring between bus stops and subway stations.

City, suburban and rural settings offer very different sorts of business, activity and lifestyle attractions. Broadly generalized, cities are stereotypically characterized as fast-paced "something is always happening" and socially "up-scale" environments that appeal to aggressive "go-getters." At the same time, they are also places inhabited by a much larger majority of people whose fast pace involves running to scrape by, along with those who have given up the race altogether.

Suburbs are broadly regarded as good and safe places to raise children surrounded by other families with shared community priorities. Prized attractions and amenities include close access to active businesses, convenience shopping and community services and high standard schools.

Rural lifestyles are in many ways opposite of urban. There's still a lot to do, but at a slower, more relaxed pace with a less distracted and simpler lifestyle. As with suburban living, a less transient "small town" environment promotes closer long-term ties to friends and neighbors, active interest and engagement in community affairs and activities structured and centered upon children and extended families.[115]

Assuming now that these broad generalizations are more true than they are flawed, how would variously prophesied smart tech promises and problems disproportionately impact each relative to the others?

Would comprehensively wired-together smart city efficiencies, on-call driverless cars and ubiquitous anti-crime surveillance monitoring be readily acceptable in more suburban and outlying locations?

Would large corporate offices downsize their metropolitan facilities and operations due to less reliance on in-house personnel and a shift to telecommuting employees and remote as-needed expertise, therein reducing their host city's real estate, business and employee tax revenues to finance those smart city updates?

Would suburbs and rural communities, in balance, gain resident populations, business start-ups and services, infrastructure investment capital and tax revenues and private and public citizen employment opportunities inherited from corporate decentralization and business exodus from high urban taxation, regulation and physical and social deterioration?

Would the more metro-independent suburbs and rural communities be less reliant upon, and thereby less negatively impacted by disruptive AI and automation developments due to availability of less expensive human labor and increasingly person-centric markets such as healthcare and community-based education programs?

How will each type of community redefine and optimize its most attractive features in order to adapt, where will the resources come from and what is the federal government's role and responsibility in supporting these transitions?

And the biggest question of all: how would variously proposed remedies to unemployment, workforce realignments and "income equity" stratification impact America's overall long-term socio-economic future?

First, let's just imagine that these urban trends, aided and abetted by technology, advance as suggested. In this scenario, major businesses will decentralize away from costly big city real estate and taxes. Telecommuting and remote consulting will extend greater elective freedom for family income providers to reside in more affordable and safer places to raise children. Growing suburban and rural human service needs, such as medicine for aging populations, will be augmented by tele-medicine, clinics and a larger abundance of health and assisted care workers. Less transient, more neighborhood-friendly communities promote civic engagement and pride.

Supported by smart city technology and ideology, get used to the idea that utonomous self-driving vehicles are racing our way. Waymo, Google's autonomous division, Tesla and Uber are currently leading the pack.

Google had been testing autonomous cars in Mountain View for years before moving its autonomous division to California's Central Valley. Uber moved its test fleet to Tempe in 2017 after a dispute with California over permitting. Uber also operates an autonomous test fleet in Pittsburgh, where it lured top computer-vision and robotics researchers from Carnegie Mellon to help it transform car services from flex work to automation.

Presently, Uber refers to driverless car drivers as "pilots" or "operators." Their role is to coax the vehicles along much like copilots or rally navigators as computers do the work. The humans hold laptops for visualization of the road ahead, which is captured by a LIDAR unit atop the vehicle. A remote-sensing laser is used for guidance, with data processed by the vehicle's onboard computers.[116]

Still, for many of us, private automobile and truck ownership remains necessary, symbolizes individual freedom and even holds a cherished history of romance.

As Eric Risberg nostalgically observes:

From the romance of the road trip to the feeling of

> *getting your driver's license, the car has always*
> *conjured images of freedom and control. Those time-*
> *worn ideals, however, may soon be a relic of the*
> *past.* [117]

Risberg reflects that our current idea of the car is based on the individual or family:

> *[I]t is personal travel, single ownership and*
> *individualism in general that fuel our car-obsessed*
> *culture. But with driverless cars, a large part of*
> *transportation and commuting could instead be*
> *thought of as an interlinked system where cars are*
> *simply moving through our streets, and then only if*
> *and when needed. As a result, the currently neat line*
> *dividing public and private transit might start to get*
> *a bit fuzzy.*

And after all, isn't this all for the good? Think about the benefits we are promised. We can still have the privacy and effectiveness of a single car for rides to a work or meeting place remote from a metro line. We can check our emails and text on the way (or whatever replaces them—newspapers will be a thing of the past), plus take along our breakfast and leave any spilled coffee and crumbs behind for the next rider to deal with.

We can be dropped off in the crowded city and be free of the vehicle along with parking space for other uses. We will also no longer need to store and maintain a thirty-or-forty-thousand-dollar machine in our garage.

But what about those of us who are, for any dumb, backward notion, still very attached to the idea of having those beast and beauty relics? Writing in *The Atlantic*, Ian Bogoost reminds us that private automobile ownership symbolizes a core American tradition of access and freedom. He writes:

*A car made any place accessible, even if just in theory.
That's also why cars became a means of self-
expression: How to go somewhere was a choice, so the
type and color of a car conveyed a style.*[118]

Bogoost then asks:

*How can a car offer freedom when you have to ask a
company to let you use it? Instead, cars will recede
into the background. They will become
infrastructure—still important, but unseen unless
they break down.*

*Nobody will care what anyone drives, no more
than they might ponder the manufacturer of elevator
cabins or subway rolling stock. It might be annoying
when the elevator takes forever or the train doesn't
come, but these matters are akin to acts of God,
conducted outside ordinary people's influence. And as
the intimate familiarity of choosing, operating, and
maintaining vehicles recedes, people will develop a
new tolerance for whatever the companies that run the
services choose, in terms of appearance and access.*

Yet let's also remember that cities offer important lifestyle and
cultural attractions that will hold enduring treasures as well.
Each is uniquely special, culturally diverse, historically
significant, energetically stimulating and organically evolving
and enriching. Perhaps noisy and congested, their residents and
endless streams of visitors encounter and celebrate wonderful
architectures and impressive centers of commerce, marvelous
world-class museums and live theater, thriving hustle and bustle
of activity and a vivid, multi-hued spectrum of humanity and
enterprise.

In any case, any technology-driven fright flight from large
cities won't happen quickly or completely. Nor will

metropolitan transformations to bright, visionary sci-fi-style centers with all-things automated and modern.

No, it won't be like that at all. Those new smart city utopian-marketed infrastructures will be built upon and around the bones and hulking shells of aging cores. Many improvements are likely to occur to the detriment of older traditions and localized lifestyles that will be left behind and displaced in exchange for technological efficiencies and conveniences.

John Steinbeck painted a grim picture of accelerating outcomes in his 1960 book *Travels with Charley: In Search of America*:

> *When a city begins to grow and spread outward from the edges, the center which was once its glory...goes into a period of desolation inhabited at night by the vague ruins of men. The lotus eaters who struggle daily toward unconsciousness by the way of raw alcohol. Nearly every city I know has such a dying mother of violence and despair where at night the brightness of the street lamps is sucked away and policemen walk in pairs.*

Perhaps more optimistically, Steinbeck then adds:

> *And then one day perhaps the city returns and rips out the sore and builds a monument to its past.*

The challenge is for human society to determine what cultural and economic monuments will represent America's future.

THE DEEP STATE OF INFOTECH DEEP POCKETS

ENORMOUS AND EVER-EXPANDING national and global power and influence wielded by information tech giants warrant judicious contemplation. As Rachael Holmes urges us to recognize:

> *The fact that billions of us now use a handful of corporate-owned global platforms to manage pretty much every aspect of our daily lives indicates how fast the potential of digital culture is shrinking. A tectonic rift exists between the corporate apparatuses of Google, Facebook, WhatsApp (now owned by Facebook), Twitter, Apple and Amazon, and the open source and creative commons ideals of the Internet of public good.*[119]

Holmes warns that we dangerously risk allowing ourselves to become a vast network of informants on each other and ourselves, a wireless connected system where GPS-based location tracks us on our mobile phones; one where social media apps monitor, record and pass along personal information about our spontaneous thoughts, social lives and connected

147

relationships; one which has no national borders; one which does not recognize outmoded distinctions between state and corporate power, citizens and consumers and platforms and products.

We have become a society of individuals who behave on a spectrum of willing complicity with the demise of our privacy. Rachael Holmes writes:

> *We know Twitter is broadcasting. We're generally naïve about limits to our visibility and history on Facebook. We're in self-denial where there ought to be reasonable expectation of privacy, as with texts, emails and online shopping. In truth we already know nothing's private because the corporates and government can get it anyway. And the icing on the cake is that we are paying for our surveillance out of our own hard-pressed pockets.*[120]

So, after all, who rules the technology?

It is those who develop the algorithms and those who control the secured gateway on ramps, toll booths and draw bridges along the Internet super highway.

The power resides with purse-string politicos and big tech companies who will hold sway over smart cities with smart cars wirelessly connected to a vast Internet of Things network which extend from our home appliances—to our places of work—to our sidewalks and streets—to electronic eyes and ears that track and display our every movement on remote facial recognition monitors.

The rulers are those who control enormously prosperous, unaccountable, ideologically and politically biased digital access and social media companies that manipulate and censor information to fit their preferred narratives.

In summary, the technology rulers are all those whom the rest of us relinquish our long-cherished rights of privacy and self-determination to. There are many of them. They are not only winning…we are generously paying them to do so.

Silicon Valley Socialism

Silicon Valley socialism marches far and wide. Monopolistic info tech behemoths with astonishing economic lobbying swag have come to exert tremendous influence over our open access to *all* public and private information and opinion discussions. Their status as corporate—rather than governmental—entities, entitles them to determine what we are allowed to see, what we are not allowed to see, and from whom, entirely at their own discretion. Moreover, they can do so without having to justify their specific-case decisions, or to explain their rationale.

British author and journalist Steven Poole asks us to consider how worried we should be regarding which vision prevails and who wields what influence over the broad personal and public aspects of our lives. Writing in *The Guardian* he urges that in contemplating our answer, we attempt to imagine the sort of lives we would be willing to accept for ourselves—or for our children and grandchildren—a decade or two from now, given the trends we are already witnessing today.

Poole writes:

> *Imagine, for example, that as soon as you step outside your door—maybe even before—your actions are swept into a digital dragnet. Video surveillance cameras placed everywhere record footage of your face which becomes entered for correlation by feature recognition algorithms matched with photos on your driver's license to a national ID database.*[121]

The reason offered for these intrusions on our privacy, of course, is that all of this is being done in our best interest to enhance our safety.

This being the case, Poole continues to question what this "best safety interest" answer has to do with allowing stealthy algorithms to keep track of what we purchase online; where we are at any given time; who our friends are and how we interact with them; how many hours we spend watching television or playing video games; and what bills we pay (or don't).

These intrusions should be quite easy to imagine because they are already occurring.

As Rachel Botsman reminds us in her book *Who Can You Trust? How Technology Brought Us Together and Why It Might Drive Us Apart*, that most of this already happens thanks to social media data-collecting behemoths. Botsman references a 2015 Office of Economic Development (OECD) study revealed that at that time there were already about one-quarter as many connected private and government-operated monitoring devices in the United States as the entire population.

Other agencies are likely to follow the National Security Agency (NSA) watchdog lead. Although the U.S. Department of Transportation Security Administration scrapped a proposal to expand PreCheck background checks to include social media records, location data and purchase history following heavy criticism, a major new terror incident can readily revive the plan. [122]

What could possibly go wrong?

Maybe consider whether you would wish to endorse the adoption of the State Council of China's 2014 document called Planning Outline for the Construction of a Social Credit System as a credo for your nation's future. As the document claims:

> It will forge a public opinion environment where keeping trust is glorious. It will strengthen sincerity in government affairs, commercial sincerity, social sincerity and the construction of judicial credibility.

In other words, trust government to ensure everyone's sincerity on all matters, particularly sincere universal approval of the credibility of its omnipotent judicial sovereignty.

Even in the United States, credit scoring is certainly not a new idea. More than 70 years ago, two Americans, Bill Fair and Earl Isaac, created the Fair Isaac Corporation (FICO), a data analytics company, to establish credit scores that can be applied by commercial companies to determine many financial decisions. These client service rankings include determinations regarding whether an applicant should be given a loan, and what interest rate should be applied to a consumer property mortgage.

Unlike the United States, at least so far, there is little if any daylight in China between government and its high-tech corporate agendas.

Paul Triolo, a technology analyst at the Eurasia Group think tank, warns of ominous global influences as Beijing leaders nationalize some of its high-tech giants into de facto instruments of the state. China's so-called "Great Firewall" is effectively creating a dilemma of two Internets with separate communication privacy standards. The firewall lets the government control the web content Chinese citizens can view. [123]

Google's China-specific search engine, Google.cn, was launched in 2006 as a means for the company to stay in the country while abiding by its strict censorship rules. The company's normal search engine was also still technically available but was heavily filtered.

Critics charge, for example, that China could use the new Dragonfly to replace air pollution information in online news reports, giving the appearance that pollution levels aren't as dangerous as they actually are.

Google eventually bailed on the project in 2010 amid China's accusations that the company allowed pornography on its search engine. A sophisticated hacking attempt on Google that originated in China was the last straw, at least temporarily prompting the company to stop censoring content there and move its operations from the mainland.

While Google says it's only exploring a new search engine for the Chinese market, the tech giant already has an existing presence in the country. China is the world's most populous country with a growing middle class which is becoming increasingly connected. Abandoning China would cede the country's huge market to homegrown competitors like Baidu, China's largest search engine.

Nevertheless, U.S. lawmakers are understandably lambasting Google for even considering working with the Chinese government again. Senator Tom Cotton (R-AR) issued a statement in August 2018, calling out the tech giant for potentially working on a new Chinese information search engine. He wrote:

> *Google claims to value freedom and one hopes Google will put its corporate principles and America first, ahead of Chinese cash.*[124]

Chinese and other Internet-connected companies are being forced to make their businesses work uniformly everywhere else they can. An influential model for accomplishing this is the General Data Protection Regulation (GDPR) enacted in 2018 under European Union law to protect the privacy of all individuals within the EU and European Economic Area (EEA).

GDPR requires that all business processes that handle personal data be designed and built with consideration of the principles and provide safeguards to protect data, using the highest-possible privacy settings to prevent outside transfer to third parties without explicit, informed consent. The data also cannot be used to identify a subject without additional information stored separately.

Some U.S. tech companies are already doing this. Microsoft Corp. said it will apply GDPR rules across all its services throughout the world. Apple Inc. has for years positioned itself as the data-protection and privacy company, and its CEO Tim Cook supports a U.S. privacy law in line with Europe's. Facebook, on the other hand, has tried to make an end run around EU rules by giving its users a stark choice: give up some rights or delete their accounts.

As reported by Kevin Williamson in the *Wall Street Journal*, Facebook has made it known that it would find it easier to operate under a single, international regulatory regime. He quotes CEO Marl Zuckerberg calling for "a more [globally] standardized approach" which is aimed vaguely at "protecting society" as a matter of thwarting "threats" to public safety."

Williamson, also a correspondent for the *National Review*, notes that Facebook is already working with European governments to craft a regulatory regime it can live with. He comments:

> That's troubling. Freedom House reports there is 'no official [Facebook] censorship'. In Austria, even as it admits that some speech, notably pro-Nazi political speech, is prohibited by law, which is the definition of official censorship. In Austria, possession of banned books can be punished with prison sentences of up to 20 years.

Other more data-dependent U.S. companies aren't eager to comply with GDPR standards either. Google is fighting efforts to export those rules. The company's official wish list on "responsible" data-protection regulation includes a "flexible" definition of personal data and no restrictions on the geographic allocation of data storage.[125]

Some of biggest tech companies currently have as much power over the hearts and minds of people as do the governments in countries where they operate. Moreover, individually and collectively, they also reach and influence more people than any other companies have in history.

Citizens, bureaucrats and politicians all over the world are now beginning to push back against that power.

Writing in the *Wall Street Journal*, Christopher Mims observes that as people become more familiar with the Internet, their views tend to change from enthusiasm to caution. This push-back against the power of digital giants also started in the West, where countries have been feeling the results of Big Tech's growing power the longest.

Mims cites a survey by the Centre for International Governance Innovation which reveals that in Kenya, for example, people are singularly positive about the impact of tech, whereas in North America and Europe, people are more concerned about overreach.

"Familiarity breeds contempt," says Fen Hampson, director of global security and politics at GIGI, who conducted the survey.[126]

The backlash is often directed at America's tech giants, such as Alphabet Inc.'s Google, Facebook Inc. and Amazon.com Inc., and how their ubiquity affects individuals and businesses. This sort of push-back will benefit burgeoning tech industries in some big countries such as China and India which can continue to dominate their large domestic markets. Tech services in many smaller countries which can't compete with the giants will be left to negotiate business roles and conditions wherever they can.

Christopher Mims views competition between large and small domestic tech companies as one that can subdivide the Internet in a way that will force the biggest players to create separate products and procedures for different regions. He foresees that the results—following a costly, complicated and protracted transition—will be better for consumers in some cases, and significantly worse in others.[127]

Global Power Plays and Push-Backs

Deadly consequences of weaponized uses of social media platforms are also prompting global support for regulatory protections. In Sri Lanka, for example, Facebook failed to heed warnings from the government and activists about its platforms serving to incite violence against the country's Muslim minority. After the country shut off access to Facebook services, the company pledged to start taking down problematic content.[128]

The Sri Lankan government's decision to shutter access to social media sites followed deadly bombs in churches and hotels that killed more than 300 people. Officials attributed some blame for the catastrophe to Silicon Valley willingness to spread falsehoods online.

The shutdown marked the second time in as many years that Sri Lanka blocked social media access out of fear that hateful misinformation postings would stoke ethnic unrest and rioting across the central part of the country. Government officials had previously done so over a week in March 2018, blocking access to Facebook and its apps, Instagram and WhatsApp, along with the messaging app Viber. Facebook was sharply rebuked for failing to act quickly to take down harmful content "used to destroy families, lives and private property."[129]

A decade earlier, Facebook, Twitter and their social media peers were positively credited with spearheading pro-democracy uprisings that toppled dictators throughout the Middle East. Their services were also seen as great benefit during natural catastrophes, allowing authorities the means to convey crucial information, and to organize assistance.

Those same social media sites are increasingly being used and accurately perceived as forces that corrode democracy as well as to promote it. Tyrants and terrorists exploit their vast public outreach capacities to spread disinformation and to fuel ethnic violence.

At the same time, and as Emma Llansó, the director of the

Center for Democracy and Technology's Free Expression Project notes, censorship laws can serve as a "pretext for enforcing against political dissidents or journalists." [130]

Facebook and Google remain banned in China. YouTube has been periodically blocked in more than two dozen countries since the service was founded, including an incident in 2007 when a Turkish court ordered the removal of videos critical of the country's founder. Russia has recently sought to criminalize the spread of "fake news."

The United Nations has linked hate speech on Facebook with the mass killings in Myanmar and a top general used the site to spread false information about the Rohingya, a Muslim minority that Myanmar authorities refuse to recognize as citizens.

European and other democratic governments have introduced new laws targeting hate speech and terrorist content. The Australian parliament, for example, passed a law under which tech executives face up to three years in prison if they don't remove objectionable content from their platforms quickly enough and with sufficient enthusiasm to satisfy political authorities.

Germany began implementing a tough online anti-hate-speech law in 2018. Tech giants have responded by lambasting the U.K. blueprint as a threat to users' ability to communicate unfettered online. [131]

Such censorship is said to be justified as streitbare Demokratie—"militant democracy," a German constitutional principle under which certain kinds of political communication are censored, and certain political parties and organizations are prohibited. This theory holds that liberal democracies must sometimes act in illiberal and antidemocratic ways to counter political tendencies that constitute threats to the liberal democratic order. [132]

Kevin Williamson warns us to recognize erosions of our American First Amendment free speech principles as this theory becomes weaponized and vulgarized under the slogan "No free speech for Nazis." The term "Nazi" can be ubiquitously applied to encompass almost everyone—ranging from radical feminists with unfashionable ideas about transgender issues to mild-mannered fellows of the American Enterprise Institute.

Williamson argues that although European practice are significantly at odds with our First Amendment, they are made somewhat more understandable when viewed in a postwar European context, one in which a revanchist Nazi movement really wasn't previously unthinkable at all. He asks us to consider that the dicey part in all of this is trying to figure out what constitutes a genuine threat:

> Is it a group of skinheads in Munich planning a pogrom? A bookseller stocking 'Mein Kampf? An anti-Semitic letter from Henry Ford? [133]

As a practical matter, Williamson predicts that eventual and perhaps inevitable government standards governing speech restrictions on tech platforms will reflect more restrictive European practice rather than more liberal American practice. He points out that the Big Tech companies will ultimately jump in line for much the same reason that California's relative stringent automotive emission standards act as an effectively national standard:

> Corporations generally prefer standardization and homogenization where they are economical.

This being the case, Kevin Williamson urges us to be clear about what regulatory standardization and homogenization mean: Official censorship by governments abroad, proxy censorship by business interests at home and doublespeak on all sides. He prudently concludes:

> *You can have streitbare Demokratie, or you can have*
> *a political culture so childish and illiterate that it*
> *can't distinguish between Charlie Kirk, Charles*
> *Murray and Charles Mansion. But you can't have*
> *both and a free society too.*[134]

Collapsing Social Media Platform Pretenses

Social media platforms hold great discretion over what information they deem appropriate to carry.

Under Section 230 of the Communications Decency Act, the U.S. Congress granted immunity from libel to online platforms such as Google, Facebook and Twitter for their users' defamatory, fraudulent or otherwise unlawful content. This exemption from standard laws and regulations applied to media publishers affords them extraordinary benefit to facilitate "forums for a true diversity of political discourse."

The designation as platforms, rather than as information publishers or producers, assumed that social media companies would operate as impartial, open channels of communication— not curators of acceptable opinions. When this distinction is no longer the case, we should carefully reconsider "neutral public forum" merits warranting special benefits.

This neutrality has all-too-often been absent, particularly with regard to conservative views. So long as this continues, the social media industry giants should be held to the same liability standards other publishers are subject to.

Still, the jackpot questions remain...what sort of regulation standards are we, the users, prepared to accept? Who would write and enforce them? Do we really want to put political government bureaucrats in charge of determining boundaries of what constitutes "hate speech" and disseminations of "false information" advertisements?

Making governments, the U.S. goverment along with others, the ultimate arbiters of truth readily conjures dystopian images of George Orwell's *1984*, and Margaret Atwood's *The Handmaid's Tale*. We are already witnessing evidence of such horrors being enacted by authoritarian regimes such as that in China which severely limit and monitor what their citizens can say and do online.

Some people commonly argue that if for-profit social media platforms serve as contemporary town squares, they are being operated as what Harvard Business School Professor Shoshana Zuboff refers to as "surveillance capitalism." In other words, they are biased and profit-driven enterprises that depend upon the accumulation and monetarization of personal data.

The flip side of this is that businesses aren't the only entities that exploit so-called town squares. They also serve as invaluable tools used by oppressive regimes and skillful politicos to gain and remain in power.

Nevertheless, even many of the staunchest proponents of private social media companies support varying sorts of government regulations. At the same time, the matter of "which sorts" they support is far from unanimous. When people begin suggesting that certain communications and expressions be regulated, they are typically referring to those "other people's" communications and expressions.

Notwithstanding broad support for curbs on corporate social media power, there is also good reason for accepted communication content will continue to depend upon those who are responsible for determining and enforcing any side of any issue. Those holding power - whether government or corporations—will control the flow of information and ideas.

There's also an all-important matter of personal responsibility in this discussion regarding how each of us must remain accountable for vetting out the sources of information we choose to believe.

Can and should regulations attempt to prevent people from being gullible? Who must determine when a social media platform has merely provided a free speech platform, or rather when they have intentionally enabled an entity to commit fraud?

Writing in *The Washington Post*, Anne Applebaum rhetorically questions who is really making up such rules of our new information network—and it isn't us.

> *It isn't citizens, or Congress, who decide how our information network regulates itself. We don't get to decide how information companies collect data, and we don't get to decide how transparent they should be. The tech companies do that all by themselves.*[135]

And why does this matter? Applebaum explains:

> *Because this is the information network that now brings most people their news and opinions about politics, about medicine, about the economy. This is also the information network that is fueling polarization, that favors sensational news over constructive news and that has destroyed the business model of local and investigative journalism.*

She adds:

> *These companies also operate according to their own rules and algorithms. They decide how data gets collected and who sees it. They decide how political and commercial advertising is regulated and monitored. They even decide what gets censored. The public sphere is shaped by these decisions, but the public has no say.*[136]

Applebaum offers a historical analog to the dilemma harking back to the 1920s and 1930s when democratic governments suddenly found themselves challenged by a new information technology called radio, whose early stars included Adolph

Hitler and Joseph Stalin. This experience demonstrated that the revolutionary instant national and global communication invention could be used to provoke anger and violence.

England responded by designing the British Broadcasting Corp., the BBC, to connect all parts of the country together into a single national conversation as well as to "inform, educate and entertain."

The United States responded in another way: one where journalists accepted a regulatory framework, a set of rules about libel law and a public process that determined who could get a radio license.

Anne Applebaum frames the current priority as seeking to find the equivalent of licensing and public broadcasting in the world of social media—to find the most appropriate and effective regulatory or social or legal measures that will make this new Internet technology work for us, for our society and our democracy, and not just for Facebook (and other social media) shareholders.

Although Applebaum offers no conclusive answers, she clarifies that her arguments do not favor government censorship to replace censorship by corporate fiat. Rather, she suggests, it is a broader argument which favors applications of the same kinds of regulations to the online world that have been used in other spheres, to set rules on transparency, privacy, data and competition. This would include regulating Internet advertising, "just as we regulate broadcast advertising, insisting that people know when and why they are being shown political ads or, indeed, any ads."

Applebaum emphasizes a need to deepen the debate on solutions:

> *[It] cannot include another chaotic, amateurish interview with Facebook chief executive Mark Zuckerberg in the Senate. Constantly changing technology will make it difficult, as will lobbying.*

> *But we have regulated financial markets, another*
> *sphere where the technology changes constantly, the*
> *money involved is enormous, everyone is lobbying,*
> *and everyone is trying to cheat.*[137]

Yet try as we may, in the end we are left with only one voting choice regarding who will make up the rules. If our choice is between government and business—and it is—only government can enforce accountability so long as huge media interests hold non-competitive monopolies.

If, on the other hand those monopolies are broken, it will require federal and state government antitrust enforcements to make this happen as well.

Having said this, it's dangerously unrealistic to authorize nanny state governments to approve everything posted online to ensure that no one is offended as an excuse to extend even more bureaucratic influences over our lives.

At the same time, we're also heading for big really big trouble if we continue to allow information and communication control by algorithms devised by enormously powerful and politically biased social media oligarchies.

Paradoxically, both options are lousy, and with no easy answers. Hence, we, all American citizens—ideologically left, right and center—face a common dilemma.

As Anne Applebaum concludes, there is a vital national interest at stake in weighing and addressing all consequences of this pressing regulation debate:

> *If we don't do it—if we don't even try—we will not*
> *be able to ensure the integrity of elections or the*
> *decency of the public sphere. If we don't do it, in the*
> *long term there won't even be a public sphere, and*
> *there won't be functional democracies anymore,*
> *either.*[138]

CYBER TRAWLERS FISHING THE INTERNET

HAVING TOUCHED UPON some of the damnably perplexing challenges in determining best ways to regulate or otherwise incentivize fairness in social media platforms, it is also vital to consider influences of any such policies in keeping America and its citizens safe from foreign and domestic cyberattacks.

A case in point involved seemingly disturbing arrangements between government, political and social media organizations connected with investigations into Russian hacking of the Democratic National Committee (DNC) during the 2016 presidential election.

In his extensive report into potential Trump campaign collusion with Russian interests, Special Counsel Robert S. Mueller noted that his team did not "obtain or examine" the DNC servers in determining whether they had been hacked by Russia. Instead, the matter was investigated by the FBI and other agencies.[139]

Remarkably, it turned out that the DNC had refused to allow the FBI access to its servers. They instead reached a special arrangement with the FBI to transfer that forensics responsibility to a third-party Google-owned company named CrowdStrike.

Breitbart reported that although a senior law enforcement official repeatedly stressed the importance of the FBI gaining direct access to the servers, a request that was denied by the DNC.

CrowdStrike had been financed by a $100 million funding drive by Google Capital, which now goes by the name of CapitalG, an arm of Google's parent company, Alphabet Inc. Eric Schmidt, CEO of Alphanet, in turn, was an active supporter of the Hillary Clinton campaign and a long-time DNC donor.

Breitbart has reported that Perkins Coie, the law firm that represented the DNC and Clinton's campaign, helped to enlist CrowdStrike to aid with the DNC's allegedly hacked server. On behalf of the DNC and Clinton's campaign, Perkins Coie also paid the controversial Fusion GPS firm to produce the infamous, discredited anti-Trump dossier compiled by former British spy Christopher Steele.

Mueller's report states that the GRU, the Main Directorate of the General Staff of the Armed Forces of the Russian Federation, "stole approximately 300 gigabytes of data from the DNC cloud-based account." [140]

The GRU also targeted "individuals and entities involved in the administration" of the presidential election, the report documents. It states:

> Victims included U.S. state and local entities, such as state boards of elections (SBOEs), secretaries of state, and county governments, as well as individuals who worked for those entities. [141]

Yet the Special Counsel's office "did not investigate further" the evidence it said it found showing that Russia's GRU targeted the DNC and the other entities. Mueller's team did not examine or obtain the DNC's servers. [142]

If Mueller's investigation had investigated further, they would have found some evidence of Russian campaign tampering after all. According to DNC officials, the "hackers" had gained the entire database of opposition research on then-GOP presidential candidate Donald Trump.[143]

Culprits Hiding in the Dark Web

While the terms "Internet" and "World Wide Web" are often used interchangeably, they are not the same. The former refers to a massive network of networks, linking millions of computers globally, where any computer can communicate with another as long as each is connected to the internet.

The World Wide Web is an information-sharing model built on top of the Internet that uses the HyperText Transfer Protocol (HTTP) which defines how messages are formatted and transmitted plus what actions web servers and browsers such as Chrome or Firefox should take in response to various commands to share information. Accordingly, the web is a large part of the Internet, but not its only component. For example, email and instant messaging are not part of the web, but rather, are part of the internet.

In this context, the web is sometimes likened to an ocean, a vast territory of unknown and inaccessible locations to the average user. An estimated 95 percent of that ocean is "invisible" to typical users on its "surface" who rely upon traditional search engines.[144]

The "visible web," which is readily accessible to general public surface surfers, consists of sites whose domain names end in .com, .org, .net, or similar variations.

The "invisible" or "hidden" web refers to all digital content that cannot be found with a search engine: information including a Gmail account, online bank statements, office intranets, direct messages through Twitter and photos uploaded to Facebook marked "private."

The invisible web isn't hidden for any inherently bad reasons. Governments, researchers, corporations, personal and political blogs, news sites, discussion forums, religious sites and radio stations, for example, go there to store content on dynamic web pages.

In fact, people regularly use deep content without realizing it…material that is dynamically produced via accessing a surface site as a unique web page seen only upon request. Examples here include travel sites such as Hotwire and Expedia which allow searchers to directly access airline and hotel databases through a query in a search box, such as the name of a destination.

The web ocean gets darker as we dive deeper.

The layer just below the surface web lies what is sometimes referred to as the "deep web," a private area that isn't accessible by typical search engines, but simply contains password-protected information that isn't available to the public. These data components include personal bank accounts, retail accounts and member-only sites and internal school or company websites.

Diving much deeper, we reach "dark web" depths which can only be accessed with specific software. This region, which comprises about 3 percent of the Internet, is a particularly popular hidden domain for criminals to lurk: a place where very stealthy thieves who remain anonymous and untraceable collect and stash private information stolen from the level above.

The dark web can be more appropriately characterized as a hidden network of websites which, unlike user IP addresses which can be traced to a computer, enable visitors to mask their true identities. This is accomplished by masking software that takes an evasive randomized path and bounces between a number of encrypted connections to its ultimate file destination.

According to a 2016 report by the European intelligence organization Intelliagg and its U.S. counterpart, DARKSUM, estimates reveal that about half of dark web content is legal under U.S. or U.K. law. However, the criminal components of the dark web are far-ranging. Illicit user activities include child pornography and sex trafficking, illegal drug connections, advertisements for services of violent hitmen and sales of fake

IDs and passports.[145]

Global networks of dark web fraudsters can gain access to valuable information such as Social Security Numbers and bank account access codes captured through data breeches and hacks. This information is often sold to third party purchasers in bundles called "Fullz" (full packages of individual private materials which may include SSNs, birth dates, account numbers and other data that can be hijacked.)

Fullz are frequently traded on the dark web repeatedly. Entire "communities" of traders even post reviews that indicate whether or not the criminal source is someone "good to do business with."

The dark web can be a very dangerous trap for unaware Internet users who allow themselves to be pulled in. According to Michael Lewis, a blog writer with Moneycrashers, "Browsing its hidden sites without precautions might be compared to trying to get safely through a village infected by Ebola." [146]

In addition to malware dangers, dark web visitors to controversially dangerous sites may invite unwanted government surveillance. This applies particularly to countries such as Iran, Syria and Turkey where browsing a government-monitored ideologically out-of-line website can get you into really big trouble.

An unceasing technology race is pitting the "good guys," who are developing tools to reveal unlawful activities, against those who are producing ever more sophisticated new generations of malware. We can thank some of the Big Tech companies for leading contributions to this ongoing defensive warfare.

At the same time, even many proponents of Internet privacy assert that the dark web is essential to protect our freedom and liberty. In support of this view, a 1997 U.S. Supreme Court decision in the case of Reno v. American Civil Liberties Union extended full First Amendment protections to the Internet, which virtually guarantees the continued existence of the dark web.

Global Bonnies and CyberClydes

"Fancy Bear," the Russian cybergroup tied to famously stealing and leaking DNC emails, wasn't new at the game of trying to influence foreign national elections. Their efforts to manipulate democracies have also been discovered in German, French, and Ukrainian campaigns.[147]

Operating under a variety of different identities, Fancy Bear is believed to be strongly associated with the Russian government and seems to support cyberwarfare activities. The organization reportedly got its start in 2008, hacking the Georgian government to throw it into chaos just before the Russian government invaded the country. Since then, they've been involved in countless controversies and conflicts in the region, doing everything from threatening anti-Kremlin journalists and protesters, hacking the German parliament for over six months in 2014, making death threats to wives of U.S. Army personnel and disabling 20 percent of Ukraine's artillery via a corrupted app.[148]

Russian cybercriminal Evgeniy Mikhailovich Bogachev certainly appears to be connected with the Russian government as well. It took the FBI and other international crime organizations two years just to get the guy's name after he had managed to infect millions of computers around the world with ransomware, steal all of their stored data and cause an estimated $100 million in damages.

Although the FBI offered three million dollars to anyone who could help bring Bogachev to justice, the Russian government has shown no interest in collecting. Although Moscow has never admitted to working with him, the cybercriminal lives openly in Anapa, a run-down resort town on the Black Sea in southern Russia with a number of luxury cars and his own private yacht.

China is establishing a form of Big Data "surveillance capitalism" the likes and scale of which the world has never seen. This ambitious enterprise includes a huge foreign espionage and hacking operation conducted by China's Unit 61398.[149]

Between 2006 and 2011, Unit 61398's operation Shadt RAT infiltrated and stole data from over foreign 70 companies, governments and non-profit organizations.

Google was hacked in 2009, in part to spy on accounts of Chinese human rights activists and other dissidents. Five years later, Beijing stole sensitive information on around 22 million people, stored at the U.S. Office of Personnel Management, who had or previously held security clearances with the U.S. government.[150]

A hacker group believed to be backed by China has targeted universities engaged in naval research in order to support the country's naval capability developments. The University of Hawaii, the University of Washington, and MIT are among the at least 27 institutions hit in the United States, Canada, and Southeast Asia.[151]

China also targets foreign engineering, transportation and defense sectors. Two of the group's techniques include web shells and spear-phishing emails. A web shell is a script that can be uploaded onto a web server to gain remote administration control over it. Phishing emails usually involves embedded emails with attachments containing malware, as well as malicious Google Drive links.

Unit 61398 has been blamed for a hack that saw sensitive documents stolen regarding Israel's missile defense system. The Unit is large, estimated to have well over a thousand servers and a massive army of online hackers.

Hacking Israel military information is a particularly big deal considering that there is likely no more sophisticated cyberintelligence organization in the world than Israel's Unit 8200.

According to Peter Roberts, a senior research fellow at

Britain's Royal United Services Institute: "Unit 8200 is probably the foremost technical intelligence agency in the world and stands on a par with the NSA [the U.S. National Security Agency] in everything except scale." [152]

Founded in 1953 as the 2nd Intelligence Service Unit, the organization has since expanded into the largest Unit in the Israeli Defense Force. While many of their activities are clandestine, a few of their exploits have slipped to the surface. For example, Unit 8200 helped to develop the Stuxnet virus aimed at Iran's nuclear plants, along with very advanced spying malware called Duqu 2.0. [153]

North Korea, a country ravaged by economic sanctions, has established a substantial infrastructure of sophisticated cyberhacking cells which primarily target corporate enterprises for financial gain. Their Bureau 121 created the WannaCry ransomeware which infected around 300,000 devices in 2017 and paralyzed more than 150 organizations.

Bureau 121's most frequent U.S. marks were targeted on Houston, an oil and gas hub, and New York City, a finance hub. Foreign attacks primarily targeted banks in Germany, Turkey and the United Kingdom. [154]

North Korea was accused of using hackers to destroy Sony Pictures Entertainment computer servers in retaliation for a comedy movie that mocked Kim Jong Un. The attack paralyzed the studio's operations, leaking embarrassing executive emails. [155]

While Iran is unlikely to match the cyber capabilities of Russia, China or even North Korea in the short term, threats posed by this third-tier actor can't be ignored.

Between 2011 and 2013, in some of their first forays into cyberwarfare, Iranian hackers cost U.S. financial institutions many millions of dollars and knocked Saudi Aramco's business operations offline for months. These operations hit more than 40 American banks, including JPMorgan, Chase and Bank of America. [156]

The March 2018 "SamSam Ransomware" cyberattack that struck the City of Atlanta and cost their taxpayers as much as $17 million was traced to two Iranian men. FBI investigators have charged that Atlanta was just one of several regions targeted by those criminals which hit more than 200 victims in locations that included Newark, New Jersey, the Port of San Diego and multiple medical centers.[157]

The heist gained the two criminals more than $6 million in ransom payments with losses to victims being over $30 million.

As then-Deputy Attorney General Rod Rosenstein reported:

> *After gaining access to computers, they remotely installed their ransomware. The ransomware encrypted the computer data, crippling the ability of the victims to operate their businesses and provide critical services to their customers.*[158]

According to the Atlanta Journal-Constitution, the City of Atlanta had received years of warnings about its cybersecurity vulnerabilities. A 2010 independent audit account had warned that the Information Technology Department "currently does not have funding for business continuity and disaster recovery plans." [159]

The Atlanta Journal-Constitution also observed:

> *The city's technology leadership appears to have been overwhelmingly focused on making Atlanta a so-called 'Smart City'—a designation for cities that emphasize information and communication technology to enhance public services such as utilities and transportation.*[160]

The newspaper went on to conclude:

However, several cyber security trade publications have highlighted how these cities are especially vulnerable to attacks because of massive interdependent computer systems that constantly communicate with each other and often aren't tested before being deployed.[161]

Gaming the Chinese Checkers

In a speech on October 1, 2018, at the Hudson Institute, a conservative think tank focused on security and economic issues, Vice President Pence called on U.S. companies to reconsider business practices in China that involve turning over intellectual property or "abetting Beijing's oppression."

He said:

For example, Google should immediately end development of the Dragonfly app that will strengthen Communist Party censorship and compromise the privacy of Chinese customers.[162]

The Dragonfly search engine would enable China to block queries for terms including freedom of speech, religion and democracy. The algorithm is also reportedly designed to link users' searches to their phone numbers. That, in turn, could make it easier for Chinese authorities to identify people searching for banned topics.

Google's China-specific search engine, Google.cn, was launched in 2006 as a means for the company to stay in the country while abiding by its strict censorship rules. The company's normal search engine was also still technically available but was heavily filtered.

Critics charge, for example, that China could use the new Dragonfly to replace air pollution information in online news reports, giving the appearance that pollution levels aren't as dangerous as they actually are.

Google eventually bailed on the project in 2010 amid China's accusations that the company allowed pornography on its search engine. A sophisticated hacking attempt on Google that originated in China was the last straw, at least temporarily prompting the company to stop censoring content there and move its operations from the mainland.

While Google says it's only exploring a new search engine for the Chinese market, the tech giant already has an existing presence in the country. China is the world's most populous country with a growing middle class which is becoming increasingly connected. Abandoning China would cede the country's huge market to homegrown competitors like Baidu, China's largest search engine.

Nevertheless, U.S. lawmakers are understandably lambasting Google for even considering working with the Chinese government again. Senator Tom Cotton (R-AR) issued a statement in August 2018, calling out the tech giant for potentially working on a new Chinese information search engine. He wrote:

> *Google claims to value freedom and one hopes Google will put its corporate principles and America first, ahead of Chinese cash.*[163]

Mr. Pence's speech was the first public White House condemnation of Dragonfly, a mobile version of Google's search engine which is being designed and tested to adhere to China's strict citizen censorship program.

During the same talk, Pence accused China of seeking to "foster a culture of censorship" in academia. In doing so, the vice president cited a speech from Yang Shuping, a University of Maryland student from China who became a target of criticism there after praising the "fresh air of free speech" in America. Ms. Yang became the victim of a firestorm of criticism on China's tightly controlled social media, and her family was harassed as well.

After concerns about Google's corporate practices lead to a revolt among the company's programmers, its CEO, Sundar Pichai, outlined new corporate guidelines for ethical principles. Issuing a blog post, Pichai wrote that Google would not produce:

- Technologies that cause or are likely to cause overall harm.
- Weapons or other technologies whose principal purpose is to cause or directly facilitate injury to people.
- Technology that gathers or uses information for surveillance violating internationally accepted norms.
- Technologies whose purpose contravenes widely accepted principles of international law and human rights.

Pichai also laid out an additional seven principles to guide the design of future AI systems:

> *AI should be socially beneficial.*
> *It should avoid creating or reinforcing bias.*
> *It should be built and tested for safety.*
> *It should be accountable. Incorporate privacy design principles.*
> *It should uphold high standards of scientific excellence.*
> *It should be made available for use.*[164]

Google's ongoing behaviors directly contradict much of that lofty rhetoric.

Google's social media censorship collaboration with China becomes ever more troubling as that country now aggressively extends its weaponization of information technology capabilities into cyberspying beyond their own borders. New Chinese cybersecurity rules give their authorities sweeping powers to inspect companies' information technology and access to proprietary information—steps that warrant deep concern of all foreign businesses dealing with China operations.[165]

Chinese police officials are now authorized to remotely access corporate networks for potential security loopholes, to copy information and to inspect any records that "may endanger national security, public safety and social order." Those categories provide carte blanche opportunities to be interpreted any way they are deemed useful.

The cybersecurity law also mandates internal security checks on technology products that are supplied to the Chinese government and to critical industries such as banking and telecommunications. Foreign companies operating in China will be held responsible for allowing prohibited information to circulate online, and Internet service providers must provide "technical support" to authorities during national security or criminal investigations.

According to William Nee, an analyst at Amnesty International:

> [The new ruling] authorization strengthens the state's authority to inspect and requires that Internet-service providers and companies using the Internet are fully complying with the government's cybersecurity prerogatives.

In addition, the law mandates that foreign companies working in China store their data in that country. This requirement enables Beijing to force the disclosure of source codes and other corporate secrets, forcing companies to prove their equipment is secure. The Chinese government can then potentially leak the information to domestic competitors.

As the *Wall Street Journal* reports:

> *The rules will do nothing to assuage foreign companies' worries about security of their property. They grant authorities access to any information related to cybersecurity—a category so broadly defined as to include just about everything.*

William Zarit, chairman of the American Chamber of Commerce in China, said:

> *It justifies for authorities the right to basically copy or access anything. It doesn't seem like companies have a choice.*

In dutiful compliance, Microsoft Corp. has opened what it calls a "transparency center" in Beijing where officials can test its products for security. Apple Inc. has started building a data center in the province of Guizhou to comply with rules requiring cloud data from Chinese customers to be stored in China.

In anticipation of the law, Amazon transferred operational control of its Beijing data center to its local partner, Beijing Sinnet. As the *Wall Street Journal* reported:

> *The following November, Amazon sold the entire infrastructure to Beijing Sinnet for about $300 million. The person familiar with Amazon's probe casts the sale as a choice to 'hack off the diseased limb.'* [166]

Chinese and other international cyber hack attack threats have come to our own neighborhood businesses and homes.

As reported by *Bloomberg Newsweek*, in 2015, Amazon began quietly evaluating a startup called Elemental Technologies, a potential acquisition to help with a major expansion of its streaming video service, known today as Amazon Prime Video. Elemental made software for compressing and formatting massive video files for different devices.[167]

Amazon Web Services (AWS) was interested at the time in using Elemental Tech for highly secure cloud servers being assembled for them by Super Micro Computer Inc. (Supermicro), a San Jose, California-based company...one of the world's biggest suppliers of server motherboards, the fiberglass-mounted clusters of chips and capacitors that act as the neurons of data centers large and small.

According to Newsweek, AWS was surprised to discover tiny microchips about the size of a grain of rice nested in some of the server motherboards that didn't belong there. Amazon reported this to authorities—bugs that had the potential to end up in the International Space Station, in DOD data centers, controlling CIA drone operations and onboard networks of Navy warships.

The insidious little chips provided hackers with stealth doorways into any network that included other altered machines—all of which had a common connection. The malware all came from China.

Since the implants are tiny, the amount of code they contain is small. Nevertheless, they are capable of doing two important things: They can tell the device to communicate with one of several anonymous computers elsewhere on the Internet that are loaded with a more complex code, and they can also prepare the device's operating system to accept this new code.

The illicit chips could do all this because they were connected to the baseboard management controller, a kind of superchip that administrators use to routinely log in to problematic servers. This gives them access to the most sensitive code, even on machines that have crashed or are turned off.

Even more, the spy chips can also alter part of that code so that the server won't check for a password, opening it up to all users. This further enables them to steal encryption keys for secure communications, to block security updates that would neutralize the attack and to open up new pathways to the Internet.

Machines can be compromised to invite security breaches in two ways. One (interdiction) involves manipulating devices while they're in transit from manufacturer to customer. The other involves seeding changes from the beginning. China has a big advantage here, since they make an estimated 75 percent of the world's mobile phones and 90 percent of PCs.

That's exactly what AWS inspectors reportedly found had happened. Two company officials reported that the illicit chips were traced to operatives from a unit of the People's Liberation Army and four Chinese computer part subcontracting companies.

The stealth chips were devised to be as inconspicuous as possible. In gray or off-white colors, they looked more like signal conditioning couplers, a common motherboard component. Slight variances in size suggested that they came from different factories.

The corrupted Supermicro computers reportedly wound up in the possession of nearly 30 companies, including a major bank and government contractors. Apple Inc., an important Supermicro customer, started removing all of its 7,000 Supermicro servers from its numerous data centers following the discovery.

Amazon denied the claims. They wrote, "On this we can be very clear: Apple has never found malicious chips, 'hardware manipulations,' or vulnerabilities purposely planted in any server."

A spokesman for Supermicro, Perry Hayes, wrote, "We remain unaware of any investigation." The FBI and Office of Director of National intelligence, representing the CIA and NSA, declined to comment.

Newsweek asserts that the companies' denials were

countered by six current and former senior national security officials, who—in conversations that began during the Obama administration—detailed the discovery of chips and the government investigation.

However, no consumer data is known to have been stolen.

According to Newsweek, the stealth chips discovered in Supermicro devices were crude compared with far more sophisticated designs an Amazon security team found in altered motherboards being assembled in AWS's Beijing facilities. In one case, the malicious chips were thin enough that they'd been embedded between the layers of fiberglass onto which the other components were attached. One person who saw pictures of the chips said that this more advanced generation of chips was smaller than a sharpened pencil tip.

(Again, Newsweek said that Amazon denies that AWS knew of servers found in China containing malicious chips.)[168]

Supermicro was delisted from the Nasdaq stock market trading in 2018.

Reuters World News reported in December 2016 that the FBI was then investigating how hackers had infiltrated computers at the Federal Deposit Insurance Corporation (FDIC), one of three federal agencies that regulate commercial U.S. banks, over several years beginning in 2010. Internal communications referred to the attacks as having been carried out by Chinese military-sponsored hackers.

The FDIC reported to Congress at least seven "major" cybersecurity incidents during 2015 or 2016.

FDIC spokeswoman Barbara Hagenbaugh declined to comment on the previously unreported FBI investigation or the hack's suspected link to the Chinese military, but she said that the regulator took "immediate steps" to root out the hackers when the security breach was discovered.[169]

In late September 2015, President Obama held a White House press conference with Chinese President Xi Jinping announcing a joint understanding that America would no longer support the theft of intellectual property to benefit Chinese companies. Newsweek reported that China was willing to offer this concession because it was already developing far more advanced and surreptitious forms of hacking founded upon its near monopoly of the technology supply chain.

Just weeks following the announcement, the Obama administration quietly raised alarm with several dozen tech executives and investors at a small, invite-only meeting organized by the Pentagon. According to an unnamed participant, Defense Department officials briefed the technologists about a recent cyberattack and asked them to think about creating commercial products that could detect hardware implants. Newsweek reported:

> Attendees weren't told the name of the hardware maker involved, but it was clear to at least some in the room that it was Supermicro, the person says.

Newsweek noted that few companies have the resources of Apple and Amazon, and it took some luck even for them to spot the problem:

> This stuff is at the cutting edge of the cutting edge, and there is no easy technological solution. You have to invest in things that the world wants. You cannot invest in things that the world is not ready to accept yet.[170]

Naked Vulnerabilities in Cyberspace

So here, once again, the discussion circles back to tradeoffs associated with delegating ever-more individual independence over our lives in exchange for promises of collective wired-together efficiency and security benefits.

Harvard Law School Professor Lawrence Lessig providently

predicted in 2000 that the Internet would become an apparatus that tracks our every move, erasing important aspects of privacy and free speech in our social and political lives. "Left to itself," he said, "cyberspace will become a perfect tool of control."[171]

There are understandable reasons why citizens tend to accept what have increasingly come to be accepted reasonable tradeoffs between gaining more security at the cost of less privacy in public venues. Many of us will recall footage from security cameras that cracked cases of the 2005 London subway and 2013 Boston Marathon bombings…and when Eric Cain was caught on camera shooting a Tulane University medical student named Peter Gold in 2015 (after Gold prevented him from abducting a woman on the streets of New Orleans).

Personal privacy becomes a much more urgent priority after it is surrendered. This loss is occurring at an incomprehensibly rapid and escalating pace.

Large data companies are already collecting data on their users and until now people had to be connected to their network to be seen. But now, so-called "smart cities" are installing CCTV and other devices into panopticons where people can be watched every moment of their lives.

As marketed and presented, the data and the algorithms processing it are benign and indifferently neutral. We citizens who are constantly being observed and recorded are simply perceived as data points…information generators in various representative nodes in a system designed around the idea of data mining our ant-like patterns of behavior.[172]

This pervasive, ever-vigilant monitoring of our collective and individual activities and habits portends some very frightening implications regarding relinquishment of our privacy and prerogatives to invisible voyeurs and agenda-driven societal power-brokers who claim to represent our best interests. As Songdo, South Korea researcher S.T. Shawayri points out, the data is never neutral, essential and objective in its nature. It is invariably "cooked" to recipe by chefs embedded within institutions with aspirations and goals.[173]

And it's beyond question that our Western nation attitudes have changed over the past century.

William Webster, a professor of public policy at the University of Stirling in Scotland, notes that the pre-World War II rhetoric about public safety was:

> *'If you've got nothing to hide, you've got nothing to fear.' In hindsight, you can trace that slogan back to Nazi Germany. But the phrase was commonly used, and it crushed any sentiment against CCTVs.*[174]

Former U.K. Deputy Prime Minister Nick Clegg has observed:

> *And basically, it's happened without any meaningful public or political debate whatsoever. Partly because we don't have the history of fascism and nondemocratic regimes, which in other countries have instilled profound suspicion of the state. Here it feels benign. And we know from history, it's benign until it isn't.*[175]

Carnegie Mellon University Professor Of Information Technology Alessandro Acquisti asks us to remember:

> *In the cat-and-mouse game of privacy protection, the data subject is always the weaker side of the game.*

Acquisti reminds us that we in America haven't been through the experience of the man in the brown leather trench coat knocking on the door at four in the morning...so when we talk about government surveillance, the resonance is different. He warns:

> *[The desire for privacy] is a universal trait among*

182

humans, across cultures and across time. You find evidence of it in ancient Rome, ancient Greece, in the Bible, in the Quran. What's worrisome is that if all of us at an individual level suffer from the loss of privacy, society as a whole may realize its value only after we've lost it for good.[176]

As Gus Hosein, executive director of Privacy International, notes:

[If] the police wanted to know what was in your head in the 1800s, they would have to torture you. Now they can just find it out from your devices."[177]

George Orwell's grim 1984 story admonition that "Big Brother is watching you" has since gained a rapidly growing number of progenies. That same year he wrote it—in 1949—an American company released the first commercially available CCTV system. Two years later, in 1951, Kodak introduced its Brownie portable movie camera.

Cities are rapidly expanding CCTV networks in the interest of public security. New York City ramped up installations following the September 2001 attacks to roughly 20,000 officially-run cameras by 2018 in Manhattan alone. In 2018, Chicago reportedly had a network of 32,000 CCTVs to help combat the inner-city murder epidemic. Thanks to federal grants, Houston, which as recently as 2005 had none, had about 900 by 2018, with access to an additional 400.[178]

An estimated 106 million new surveillance cameras are now currently being sold annually in the United States. Tens of thousands of cameras known as automatic number plate recognition devices, or ANPRs, hover over roadways to catch speeding motorists and parking violators.[179]

That surveillance follows us everywhere and from everywhere.

More than 1,700 satellites monitor our planet. From a distance of about 300 miles some can discern a herd of buffalo or stages of a forest fire.

Our skies have become cluttered with drones. About 2.5 million were reportedly purchased by American hobbyists and businesses in 2016. This doesn't include a huge fleet of unmanned aerial vehicles used by the U.S. government against terrorists and illegal immigrants.

Cameras connected with facial recognition are being used to by Transportation Safety Administration (TSA) air marshals to trail and closely monitor unsuspecting Americans targeted for special airport inflight surveillance.

As reported by the Boston Globe, TSA's "Quiet Skies" program, which began in 2010, entitles and enables teams of undercover agents to document whether targeted individuals "change clothes or shave while traveling, abruptly change direction while moving through the airport, sweat, tremble or blink rapidly during the flight, use their phones, talk to other travelers or use the bathroom, among many other behaviors." [180]

The targets are not necessarily people who have done anything that warrants any previous reasons to be on a terrorist watch list, although it is intended to identify those who "flag" reasons for concern. The first red flag is foreign travel—specifically, frequent visits to "countries that we know have a high incidence of adversarial actions."

Risk assessment targeting is far from reliable. The Globe reports that a flight attendant and a federal law enforcement officer are among those who have been flagged for surveillance under the program. [181]

Personal monitoring devices are proliferating...dash cams, cyclist helmet devices to record collisions, doorbells equipped with lenses to catch package thieves and inexpensive sound and movement-activated home security cameras are becoming ubiquitous.

As Rachel Holmes accurately observes in her *Guardian*

article, it's now clear that the digital world has evolved into a creature of control. We realize that we are being watched, monitored and recorded and don't seem to care.

Facebook and other corporate Internet giants gather data to maximize profits from our consumer habits, from grocery shopping to TV viewing patterns to political interests and affiliations. Holmes writes:

> *Just like trawlers with dragnets, all sorts of other collateral data gets hauled in along the way. Data surveillance, once intangible and invisible, now blatantly announces its presence in our everyday lives. Mobile accessories and interconnectivity between gadgets and appliances in our homes—the Internet of Things—create an unprecedented network of tracking devices capturing data for commerce and government.*[182]

Holmes points out that the technology we thought we were using to make life more efficient started using us some time ago, and it's now attempting to reshape our social behaviors into patterns reminiscent of the total surveillance culture. She writes:

> *In an increasingly online everyday life, our use of social media has become a medium for normalizing the acceptability of intrusion and behavioral connection. We are bombarded by 'helpful recommendations' on education, health, relationships, taxes and leisure matched to our tracked user profiles that nudge us towards products and services to make us better citizen consumers. The app told us that you only took 100 steps today. The ad for running shoes will arrive tomorrow.*

At the same time, we appear always ready to entrust that new technology with previously unimaginable judgment determinations that directly impact our lives and loved ones. Think self-driving cars, for example, where we will be asking computer algorithms to make a split-second decision to either save the car occupants or a school bus just ahead.

And will these pilotless systems and the operators who control them be able to prevent hackers and cybercriminals from sabotaging individual vehicles or even entire fleet networks? Jeff Williams, chief technology officer of the security firm Contrast Security, warns:

> *Nobody today designs cars to operate on the internet, but all of a sudden we are connecting them. And so then we are getting thrown in the deep end....When you start adding technologies like Uconnect and all of a sudden your car is connected directly to the Internet and your car's IP address, then you are accessible from any computer in the world. We have networked all these things and now they are remotely attackable.*[183]

Williams adds:

> *If you take something that was designed to work in one set environment and you connect to it a much more hostile environment, you don't have the right defenses in place. So of course it's vulnerable. It's like Bambi walking out of the forest into the field.*
>
> *While researchers have been the primary ones to expose these weaknesses, it's only a matter of time before nefarious hackers catch on and figure out a way to make money off exploiting these dangerous vulnerabilities. Then we could potentially have a big problem on our hands.*

In 2015, security researchers Charlie Miller and Chris Valasek executed a wireless hack on a Jeep Cherokee, changing the radio station on the car's radio center, turning its windshield wipers and air conditioner on, stopping the accelerator from working, and even shutting down its engine on a St. Louis highway. Miller and Valasek were able to infiltrate the car's network through Chrysler's in-vehicle connectivity system, UNconnect.

In 2017, for the second year in a row, a group of Chinese hackers was able to demonstrate a software exploit within a Tesla vehicle, allowing them to take control of a Model X's brake system, audio and door systems. Luckily, these hackers were on our side, working to show the vulnerabilities in poorly secured software.[184]

Nevertheless, let's fully assume that autonomous vehicles will demonstrate high levels of safety and efficiencies, and that many people, most particularly those who live in or commute to cities, will benefit. Writing from Tempe, Uber's primary test city, Ian Bogoost then ponders what ways these big-corporation-owned driverless marvels will change not only the customer experiences but urban cultural experiences as well.

Bogoost urges us to realize that these new technologies are *not* simply tools that help us accomplish existing goals, like getting to the grocery store or commuting to work. They are changing how we think of space, our concepts of urban design and even the ways we relate to the world.

It is impossible for each of us to fully know what it will be like to live with primary dependence on automated taxi services. While they will free some people from certain risks and burdens of transportation, they and others will simultaneously be bound to new burdens when we allow these technology services to take control of cities.

Bogoost contemplates:

> *So much of the American city is taken up by roads filled with cars filled with people. A huge cultural*

shift will take place if all that space gets ceded to a few technology companies. Not just big things, but small ones too, like standing on medians and waiting at curbs and perceiving of different colors and styles. Tiny experiences like these frame the contours of daily life in subtle ways. [185]

In addition to sketching out the technological, ecological, health and civic impacts of self-driving cars, Bogoost ponders what it will be like to live with them when they cease to be uncanny and just become normal elements of the urban texture. Describing his personal observation, he writes:

[T]he age of autonomous cars has felt abstract and hypothetical, so far——the stuff of splashy corporate demonstrations and tech-guru prognostications, not everyday life...But standing inches away from the robot Uber, I'm hit for the first time by the tangible, ordinary reality of the future. This isn't a test track or a promotional video. This is a self-driving car in the belly of car-loving, suburban America.

Bogoost adds:

It seems clear that cars will always have a place in America. But until now, they have been slaved to the people who drive them. The roads have always belonged to people, even if those people were assumed to be inside automobiles. When that coupling is broken for good, and everywhere, the roads will likely be safer, cleaner, and more efficient. But the urban experience, especially in cities like this one [Tempe], will change forever.

But then let's reconcile ourselves to recognizing that it will change anyway—and for many inevitably interconnected technological, cultural and economic reasons—just as societies and cities always have. Perhaps it's high time to get used to that idea.

REINVENTING OUR CONCEPTS OF HUMANITY

BOTH FOR BETTER and also, very likely for worse, we are experiencing the earliest beginnings of a transformational information and cultural revolution which will impact lives of current and future generations in many ways that are presently both unpredictable and unimaginable.

One driving force behind this phenomenon—artificial intelligence—is changing not only the way we work, not only the way we think about work, but even the way we think about ourselves with regard to personal and societal values.

As Christof Koch, chief scientist and president of the Allen Institute of Brain Science in Seattle, predicts, sweeping influences of AI signal a fourth industrial revolution. He observes:

> The first, powered by the steam engine, moved us from agriculture to urban societies. The second, powered by electricity, ushered in mass production and created consumer culture. The third, centered on computers and the Internet, shifted the economy from manufacturing into services.[186]

Koch points out that before modern farm equipment and tractors came along, it took 30 times more people to farm one hundred acres than it does today. This has resulted in producing more food for growing populations at affordable prices.

Some experienced tech industry participants and observers are less sanguine about the future. Former Google China President and present Sinovation CEO Kai-Fu Lee points out that "not all inventions are created equal." [187]

Writing in the *Wall Street Journal*, Lee agrees that while many techno-optimists and historians would argue that productivity gains from new technology almost always produce benefits throughout the economy, creating more jobs and prosperity than before, this one involves far more than a single innovation, type of labor or industry.

Lee observes that whereas the calculator replaced one kind of labor, and the cotton gin disrupted an entire industry, this revolution will drive changes across hundreds of industries:

> *In the past three centuries, we've only really seen three such inventions: the steam engine and electrification created more jobs than they destroyed, in part by breaking down the work of one craftsman into simpler tasks done by dozens of factory workers.* [188]

This new revolution is already proving far more expansively impactful than previous industry workforce and workplace disruptions. Made possible by AI, the Internet has provided both a limitless platform for global information transfer and social communications, while simultaneously affording instruments for free speech and privacy infringements by the overlords.

Internet and World Wide Web organizations are rushing to implement AI, machine learning, automation and sophisticated tactical algorithms to accomplish more and more decision-critical tasks that formerly resided in human domains and brains.

Abdicating Decisions to Algorithm Designers

Algorithm-based systems never stop learning from previous decision performance lessons. As such, model-based businesses are far more than simply data-driven businesses. In model-based businesses, the continuously upgraded algorithms play important roles in defining those businesses. In a data-driven business the data helps a business, but in a model-driven business, the models are the business.

Some of the smartest and most economically impactful computer business models fundamentally rule decisions in corner offices and trading floors on Wall Street.

The days when traders bought everything from stocks and bonds to bundled credit card debt and oil based upon information tips and instincts are largely gone. That was a time when Morgan Stanley chief John Mack would tell his traders "There's blood in the water. Let's go kill." They did, and they were richly rewarded for it.[189]

Today, much of that market warfare is being accomplished by clever software with snippets of code. Algorithms monitor and predict who and what is moving the market, which companies are best positioned to win and lose and which are most desperate and vulnerable for a profitable takeover. They keep tabs on the banks' positions, value complex instruments known as derivatives, generate price quotes for clients, match buyers and sellers and flag unseen risks. They can predict how a drop in the U.S. dollar might affect corn prices, or how to value a loan to Ferrari if the Italian government raises interest rates.

As Liz Hoffman and Telis Demos explain in their *Wall Street Journal* article "Trading Places," the rise of automation occurred partly in response to trading scandals following a 2008 market meltdown. The financial crisis encouraged banks to take discretion away from error-prone and ego-driven humans. We seem to be heading to a point when our entire U.S. economy is being controlled by bots.[190]

But those algorithms, smart as are, haven't proven infallible so far either. A May 6, 2010 "flash crash" caused by algorithms caused prices of U.S. stock market shares to fall 6 percent in 5 minutes.

Although financial turbulence always has and always will be a market risk, computer algorithmic-driven trading strategies are controlling asset prices as never before.

According to Steen Jakobsen, chief investment officer at Saxo Bank, there's a simple rule of thumb that as long as the market isn't down more than 5-6 percent over two-three days: "everything will be fine and volatility will tail off." But a fall more than 6-7 percent on consecutive closes means everyone has to scramble for cover and protection.

Jacobsen warns that this is a big source of danger. The "algos," risk parity funds, ETFs, commodity trading advisors (CTAs) and volatility strategies are all positioned the same way. In many ways, the biggest risk to the market is the market itself.[191]

It can be even more risky when those algorithms are not positioned the same way—conditions when they are designed to deceive or fight one another into making bad decisions.

Trading algorithms like the Volume-Weighted Average Price (VWAP) allow companies to buy massive volumes of shares in lots of small chunks so that other traders aren't tipped off to hone-in on the action with their own buys that drive up the price.[192]

Some warring algorithms are programmed to actually prey on other algorithms. Through a process of "algo-sniffing," they are designed to detect the signature of a big VWAP in order to purchase a particular corporation's shares—then buy them faster than the VWAP and sell them to the VWAP at a profit. Although VWAP users condemn algo-sniffing as unfair, it remains legal. This has led to a growing business in adding "anti-gaming" features to execution algorithms to make their use more difficult.

Another even more devious set of strategies work to fool other algorithms through "layering" or "spoofing." A spoofer, for instance, might buy a block of shares and then issue a large number of buy orders for the same shares at prices just fractions below the current market price. This then fools other algorithms and human traders into seeing far more orders to buy the shares in question compared with the number of orders to sell them, thereby concluding that their price is going to rise.

The same spoofer might then buy the shares themselves, causing the price to rise. When it does so, the spoofer would cancel its buy orders in order to profit from the owned shares it sells.

Although it isn't at all clear that automated trading is any more dangerous than the human trading it is replacing, we are still left with a sense at the end that we have entered an era of machines—and those who own them—are controlling everything.

Those entities which control AI and information technologies will determine employment winners and losers.

Companies with more data and better algorithms will gain ever more users and data. This monopolistic self-reinforcing winner-take-all cycle will lead to God-like controls over all segments of society unknown in human history. Their instruments of power include dominion over information access and censorship, individual and business privacy, physical and economic security, transportation and energy infrastructures and financial levers of political influence which are growing at an astounding rate.

As we increasingly trust AI and the Internet of Things to run our cities, our lives and our movements, we are increasingly letting them run our corporate business economies as well

Actually, we don't have to wait for this to occur. They are already influencing the national stock market, making major strategic decisions in a wide variety of industrial operations and earning huge profits for Big Data service providers.

The Weaponization of AI and the Internet

As Steven Cohen and Matthew Granade discuss in a *Wall Street Journal* article titled "Models Will Rule the World," most of today's industry-leading companies are software model-driven companies. Not all of them started out that way...Aptiv and Domino's Pizza, for instance, are longstanding leaders in their sectors that have adopted their proprietary internal computer software to maintain or extend their competitive dominance.[193]

Model-driven businesses primarily operate based on decision framework platforms with logic derived by algorithms from data, rather than being explicitly programmed by a programmer or implicitly conveyed via individual intuition. The outputs provide predictions upon which decisions are made. Once created, a model can learn from its successes and failures with speed and sophistication that humans usually can't match.

Building such systems requires a combination of capabilities and steps: a program (often software-based) to collect desired data, processes to create models from the data, the models themselves and a mechanism (also often software-based) to deliver or act on the suggestions from those models. The predictive results are then applied to power key business decisions, such as ways to create or optimize revenue streams and to improve cost efficiencies.

Writers Huw Price and Jean Tallinn ask in their *Conversation* article blog if it is necessarily a bad thing if computers become as smart, or smarter, than humans. They point out that the narrow list of AI application successes so far is mostly useful.

They observe:

> *A little damage to Grandmasters' egos, perhaps, and a few glitches on financial markets, but it's hard to see any sign of impending catastrophe...*[194]

Price and Tallinn believe that greatest AI concerns stem from the possibility that computers might take over domains that are critical to controlling the speed and direction of technological progress itself. They ask: "What happens if computers reach and exceed human capacities to write computer programs?"

The first person to consider this possibility was Cambridge-trained mathematician IJ Good. In 1965 he observed that having intelligent machines develop even more intelligent machines would leave the human levels of intelligence far behind. He called the creation of such machine "our last invention."

In this scenario, the moment computers become better programmers than we do will mark a point in history where the speed of technological progress shifts from the speed of human thought and communication to the speed of silicon.

This is a version of Vernor Vinge's "technological singularity"—where beyond this point, the curve is driven by new dynamics and the future becomes radically unpredictable. The former San Diego State University mathematical science professor wrote that whether or how humans will be part of future superintelligence—or what it will ultimately mean to people, cannot presently be known. He compared attempting to explain the technology developed in the posthuman future of artificial intelligence as being like trying to explain Plato's Republic to a mouse.[195]

Price and Tallinn argue that even if we don't accept the premise of a looming technological singularity—that theoretical point at which AI will outstrip all human intelligence—AI will continue to play increasingly central roles in our everyday lives. Whereas various authorities in the software arena continue to debate the possibility of a "strong AI" (artificial intelligence that matches or exceeds human intelligence), a large caravan of "narrow AI" (AI that's limited to particular tasks) races steadily and speedily forward.

One by one, computers are taking over domains that were previously considered off-limits to anything but human intellect and intuition.

The late Stephen Hawking has warned that artificially intelligent machines could even kill us when they become too clever. Responding to a question during his first Ask Me Anything session on Reddit, he said:

> *The real risk with AI isn't malice but competence. A super intelligent AI will be extremely good at accomplishing its goals, and if those goals aren't aligned with ours, we're in trouble.*
>
> *You're probably not an evil ant-hater who steps on ants out of malice, but you're in charge of a hydroelectric energy project and there's an anthill in the region to be flooded, too bad for the ants. Let's not place humanity in the position of those ants.*[196]

Hawking proposed that there is no limit to what human intelligence can create:

> *[We] evolved to be smarter than our ape-like ancestors, and Einstein was smarter than his parents.*[197]

He predicts that our human AI self-learning inventions will lead to "machines whose intelligence exceeds ours by more than ours exceeds that of snails."

How soon might this happen? Hawking said he had no idea and warned not to trust "anyone who claims to know for sure that it will happen in your lifetime or that it won't happen in your lifetime. But when it happens, "it's likely to be either the best or worst thing ever to happen to humanity, so there's huge value in getting it right." [198]

As such, Hawking urged that we must "shift the goal of AI from creating pure undirected artificial intelligence to creating beneficial intelligence." [199]

Frankensteins, or Einsteins?

Critical uncertainties regarding ultimate threats posed by this new AI Frankenstein monster may revolve less around our mastery of its invention, or its mastery over us, and far more about who will ultimately master control over both.

It shouldn't be too difficult to imagine scenarios where monster inventions such as self-learning AI algorithm antagonists go righteously rogue on their tinkering technicians?

Actually, someone already thought about this a couple of centuries ago.

In Mary Shelley's famous 1818 novel, Dr. Frankenstein created intelligent life out of inanimate matter—and unfortunately too late, regretted meddling with nature.

After all, much like many view AI today, even though the monster possessed moral and emotional sensibility, society unfairly and violently rejected its appearance and strength out of fear.

Despite good intentions and deeds, the poor creature just couldn't seem to win public support. As the monster described himself, "my life has been hitherto harmless and in some degree beneficial." He even used "extreme labour" to rescue a young girl from drowning, but no matter what he did, those actions were always misinterpreted. The public assumes that he was trying to murder the girl, and William Frankenstein even assumes that his monstrous creation plans to kill him.

Perhaps immodestly, the monster had a very good opinion of his superiority over his mortal detractors. He said:

> *I was not even of the same nature as man. I was more agile than they and could subsist upon coarser diet; I bore the extremes of heat and cold with less injury to my frame; my stature far exceeded theirs.*

Mary Shelley, the monster's real-life creator, understood our natural tendency to fear what we do not understand. She wrote: "Nothing is so painful to the human mind as a great and sudden change." As Victor Frankenstein lamented:

> *I started from my sleep with horror; a cold dew covered my forehead, my teeth chattered, and every limb became convulsed: when, by the dim and yellow light of the moon, as it forced its way through the window shutters, I beheld the wretch—the miserable monster whom I had created.*

Nevertheless, that fearsome creature conjured by Mary's imagination warned that unfairly pre-judged resistance to change would portend dire consequences. The monster cried out:

> *Shall each man find a wife for his bosom, and each beast have his mate, and I be alone? I had feelings of affection, and they were requited by detestation and scorn.*
>
> *Man! You may hate, but beware! Your hours will pass in dread and misery, and soon the bolt will fall which must ravish from you your happiness forever. Are you to be happy while I grovel in the intensity of my wretchedness?*
>
> *You can blast my other passions, but revenge remains—revenge, henceforth dearer than light or food! I may die, but first you, my tyrant and tormentor, shall curse the sun that gazes on your misery. Beware, for I am fearless and therefore powerful.*

Having been warned that acting against the monster's wishes would cause him to lose everything, including his good reputation, Victor recognizes that the danger to the world is greater than consequences to himself. Accordingly, he chooses to sacrifice himself to atone for his hasty rush into scientific inquiry.

Frankenstein-like theories regarding fears and fortunes of AI-driven monsters are subjects of contentious debate in today's scientific, technological, philosophical and public policy communities. Here, as in the past, our attention drifts to extremely contrasting and divided visions which are most dramatic rather than most likely.

One of the best-known members of the dystopian camp, Elon Musk, has called Super-intelligent AI systems "the biggest risk we face as a civilization," comparing their creation to "summoning the demon." Some sharing his view warn that when humans create self-improving AI programs whose intellect dwarfs our own, we will lose the ability to understand or control them.

Utopians, on the other hand, are more inclined to expect that once AI far surpasses human intelligence, it will provide us with near-magical tools for alleviating suffering and realizing human potential. Some holding this vision foresee that super-intelligent AI systems will enable us to comprehend presently unknowable vast mysteries of the Universe, and to solve humanity's most vexing questions such as eradication of diseases, natural resource depletion and world hunger.

Both of these scenarios would require that our AI developments lead to "artificial general intelligence" which can handle the incredible diversity of tasks accomplished by the human brain. Whether or not this will ever happen, much less how those tasks will be transformed and when, remain to be pure conjecture.

Former Google China President Kai-Fu Lee doubts that achieving artificial general intelligence is "right around the corner" based upon technologies that exist today. He believes that making this jump would require several fundamental scientific breakthroughs, each of which may take many decades, if not centuries.[200]

Lee also predicts that while the real battles that lie ahead will lack the apocalyptic drama of Hollywood blockbusters, they will inevitably disrupt the structure of our economic and political systems all the same. Writing in the *Wall Street Journal*, he says:

> *This unprecedented disruption requires no new scientific breakthroughs in AI, just the application of existing technology to new problems. It will hit many white-collar professionals just as hard as it hits blue-collar workers.*

Lee adds that he remains hopeful despite immense challenges:

> *If handled with care and foresight, this AI crisis could present an opportunity for us to redirect our energy as a society to more human pursuits: to taking care of each other and our communities. To have a chance of forging that future, we must first understand the economic gauntlet that we are about to pass through.*

Will our human story end in tragedy of Frankenstein proportions, or will we be able to advance and evolve with marvelous new capacities to attain presently unfathomable superhuman accomplishments?

In either case, there is no way to turn back the clock of progress where even Einstein's space-time continuum takes on a new dimension of meaning. Unlike the speed of light, there are no known theoretical limits to computational intelligence.

Whereas the computational power of the human brain is largely prewired by evolution, AI capacities arising from revolutionary computer technology power and applications are growing exponentially.

Larry Bell

Bio-Over-Lording Ourselves

Michael Bess, Vanderbilt University professor and author of "Our Grandchildren Redesigned: Life in a Bioengineered Society," foresees a human future that is both terrifying and promising. In an interview with Vox.com contributor Sean Illing, Bess raises special concerns regarding AI's social influences on society and its ultimate potential to enable biological reengineering of our lives altogether.[201]

Bess acknowledges that people have panicked about impacts of new information technologies since the invention of the printing press.

Even long before that, Socrates argued that reading a manuscript was nowhere near as insightful as talking with its author:

> [Written words] seem to talk to you as though they were intelligent, but if you ask them anything about what they say, from a desire to be instructed, they go on telling you the same thing forever.[202]

Now, the advent of smartphones, computers and the Internet seem to be comparable in their impact to other big revolutions in communications and transportation that we've experienced over the past thousand years.

Bioengineering, however, is different. The impact of social media will pale in comparison to potential revolutions in AI or gene editing technologies. Bess projects that we're now on the verge of developing DNA-altering technologies that are so qualitatively different and more powerful that they will force us to reassess what it means to be human:

> Bioelectric implants, genetic modification packages— the ability to tamper with our very biology—this stuff goes far beyond previous advances, and I'm not

202

sure we've even begun to understand the implications.

What's more, such capabilities are advancing at an unprecedented rate. Bass observes:

> *We went from having no World Wide Web to a full-blown World Wide Web in 20 or 25 years—that's astonishing when you consider how much the Internet has changed human life. In the case of, say telephones that took many decades to fully spread and become as ubiquitous as it is today.*
>
> *So what we've seen with the Internet is blisteringly fast compared to the past. For most of human history, the world didn't change all that much in a single lifetime. That's obviously not the case anymore, and technology is the reason why.*[203]

Bess worries that mankind doesn't have enough time to adapt to these changes...adequate time to alter our habits and to reappraise our cultural sense of who we are:

> *When these things happened slower in previous eras, we had more time to assess the impacts and adjust. That is simply not true anymore. We should be far more worried about this than we are.*

Sean Illing observed that our technology is developing much faster than our culture and institutions, and that this growing gap will eventually destabilize society. Here, Bess was less pessimistic:

> *I think overall, as a society, we're insufficiently equipped, but that doesn't mean there aren't plenty of voices out there speaking sanity. What's interesting is that you can use these new technologies to get in*

> touch with those voices and connect with other people
> who are questioning these technologies. The ability to
> connect in that way offers a lot of promise if it's used
> wisely.

Professor Bess added that while many young people appear to be walking around college campuses mindlessly staring at their phones, it's clear that even they understand what's happening and why it's problematic:

> The more you live through screens, the more you're
> living in a narrow bandwidth, an abstract world
> that's increasingly artificial. And that virtual world
> is safe and controllable, but it's not rich and
> unpredictable in the way the real world is. I'm
> worried what will happen if we lose our connection to
> reality altogether.

What's most striking about us humans, Bess observes, is that we are unpredictable in very basic ways. We're more complex than we can fathom, and there's something about us that is the opposite of artificial. It's the opposite of something made:[204]

> All this genetic modification technology has the
> potential to take us into very worrisome territory
> where all the things we hold dear in our current
> world, all the values that give our lives meaning, are
> at risk. Either our survival is at risk or we become
> semi-machines who are like the marionettes of our
> own moment-to-moment experience. What becomes of
> autonomy? What becomes of free will? All these
> questions are on the table.

Bess urges each of us to ask ourselves:

> *What does it mean for a human being to flourish?*
> *These technologies are forcing us to be more deliberate*
> *about asking that question. We need to sit down with*
> *ourselves and say, 'As I look at my daily life, as I look*
> *at the past year, as I look at the past five years, what*
> *are the aspects of my life that have been the most*
> *rewarding and enriching? What things have made me*
> *flourish?'*

Bess concludes:

> *If we ask these questions in a thoughtful, explicit*
> *way, then we can say more definitely what those*
> *technologies are adding to the human experience and,*
> *more importantly, what they're subtracting from the*
> *human experience.*[205]

Ratcheting up the bioengineering potentials even farther, what if artificial intelligence begets artificial life? Such an idea is no longer an implausible script of science fiction fantasy.

As explained in the *Stanford Encyclopedia of Philosophy*, artificial life (Alife) is an outgrowth of AI technology to simulate or synthesize life functions:

> *The problem of defining life has been an interest in*
> *philosophy since its founding. If scientists were to*
> *succeed in discovering the necessary and sufficient*
> *conditions for life and then successfully synthesize it*
> *in a machine or through synthetic biology, then we*
> *would be treading on territory that has significant*
> *moral impact.*[206]

One form of ALlife, which was inspired by the work of mathematician John von Neumann, aims to achieve computational models which produce self-replicating cellular automata called "Loops." So far, these ALlife applications are content to create programs that simulate life functions rather than demonstrate "intelligence." A primary moral concern here is that these programs are designed to self-reproduce and in a way that resembles computer viruses. Successful Alife programs can potentially become computer malware vectors.

A second form of ALlife is based upon manipulating actual biological and biochemical processes in such a way that it produces novel life forms not seen in nature. It is much more morally charged.

In May 2010, scientists at the J. Craig Venter institute were able to synthesize an artificial bacterium called JCVI-syn1.0. Referred to as "Wet ALlife," this development tends to blur boundaries between bioethics and information ethics, potentially leading to dangerous bacteria or other disease agents, just as software viruses infect computers.[207]

Some even argue that information is a legitimate environment of its own which possess intrinsic value that is in some ways similar to the natural environment, while in other ways foreign. Either way, they propose that information, as is on its own a thing, is worthy of ethical concern.[208]

It's tempting to imagine that the self-learning AI-powered intellects we create that surpass our human mental capacities would still be much like us in important respects. They would just be a lot cleverer. The same hope might prevail as we humans, with the help of smart implants and bioengineered artificial DNA, evolve (or perhaps devolve) into a new posthuman variant of our current precursor model.

If so, what about those nostalgic things we may trade in for the upgraded version? Things we tend to value such as capacities for love and compassion, experiencing inspiration and joy, even mortal survival? Such characteristics are all shared with histories that have given rise to evolutions of other "higher animals."

The good news here might be that while intelligent machines and updated versions of ourselves might not share our current values, they might also lack tendencies towards hostility, another frequent expression of animal emotion.

The bad news is that if we only succeed in creating super-intelligent psychopaths, creatures without moral compasses, we probably won't be their masters for long.

Nevertheless, writing in TheConversation.com, Huw Price and Jean Tallinn point out that the same concern applies to corporations as psychopaths when they aren't sufficiently reined in by human control. The pessimistic prospect here is that AI might be similar, except much, much, cleverer, and also much faster.[209]

Price and Tallinn offer some good advice in this regard:

> A good first step, we think, would be to stop treating intelligent machines as the stuff of science fiction, and start thinking of them as a part of the reality that we or our descendants may actually confront, sooner or later.

Price and Tallinn optimistically conclude that the future isn't yet fixed, but that such optimism will only be warranted if we take the trouble to make the future an optimistic one by investigating the issues and thinking hard about the safest strategies:

> We owe it to our grandchildren—not to mention our ancestors, who worked so hard for so long to get us this far—to make that effort.[210]

Channeling Creative Destruction

Austrian economist Joseph Schumpeter coined the term "creative destruction" to characterize the way technological progress in the late 1940's improved the lives of many, but inevitably, at the expense of a smaller few. As improvements to manufacturing processes such as assembly lines benefited the general economy and overall individual lifestyles, craft and artisan producers were displaced.

Once again, many people worry that this new information revolution will have innumerable and far-reaching disruptive effects on society—putting people out of work, adding to work and income inequality and some will say, even pose an existential risk to the long-term future of Homo sapiens.

Others will remind us that just as all of the previous technical revolutions profoundly increased human productivity, welfare and lifespans, AI will make human society better. While some industries and work roles will again fall as casualties, they will be replaced by even greater, more open-ended opportunities which will require and enable more people to think smarter.

There is a natural tendency to impose bias that assumes that tomorrow will resemble our positive and negative experiences today, only a little bit different—or maybe extremely so—instead of recognizing that we are in the middle of an unknowably disruptive change.

AI, automation and the Internet are already dramatically impacting our lives in large and small ways that are legitimately argued as both good and bad. Moreover, the progeny of this triumvirate of Frankenstein monsters will continue to multiply to exert more and more influence over ever-broader aspects of our lives at an accelerating rate.[211]

Smart technology will increasingly disrupt traditional structures of our social and economic lives. Key among these impacts we might anticipate widening workplace wealth gaps and broad-spread challenges to the maintenance of personal dignity.

Social culture has trained most of us to tie our personal worth to the pursuit of work and success. It will be painful for those who watch algorithms and robots replace them at tasks they have spent years mastering and proudly attending. Many will witness those tasks and entire industries disappear altogether, as ill-fated buggy whip manufacturers experienced following the invention of the internal combustion engine.

Nevertheless, dystopian visions of massive AI-driven job losses are premature. This book began with no doomsday preconceptions regarding AI, nor does it conclude with one.

Dr. Kai-Fu Lee, author of "AI Superpowers: China, Silicon Valley and the New World Order," argues that unprecedented disruptions applying existing AI technology to new problems will hit many white-collar professionals just as hard as it hits blue-collar factory workers. Still, he says:

> *Despite these immense challenges, I remain hopeful. If handled with care and foresight, this AI crisis could present an opportunity for us to redirect our energy as a society to more human pursuits: to taking care of each other and our communities. To have any chance of forging that future, we must first understand the economic gauntlet that we are about to pass through.*[212]

Lee concludes his article optimistically:

> *Artificial Intelligence will radically disrupt the world of work, but the right policy choices can make it a force for a more compassionate social contract.*

AI and Internet-enabled systems should be recognized overall as human capacity enhancers rather than competitors. From this perspective, AI isn't an invention so much as a human tide of innovative progress in many integrative information management and system technology fields. As such, its machine learning feature allows computers to stimulate—and even expand—the way the human mind processes data.[213]

Granted, Whyte acknowledges that computers are learning to compete very rapidly. She notes that by 1997 they were better than humans at chess. Ten years later they were better at driving cars than the average teenager, and they are now better at playing at Chinese game Go, rated 300 times harder than chess.

Whyte quotes Lay Klein, chief technology officer at Voyager Labs:

> *Every time there's an advancement, we are using that as a ladder to our next step of evolution as human beings. If you look back at the Industrial Revolution, the world didn't stop after some inventions were being made. On the contrary, we continued to evolve.*

CEO and co-founder of Databricks, Ali Ghodsi, doesn't foresee a completely automated future with the human out of the loop any time soon:

> *The way AI is being built is simply not at all in any way the way true human intelligence works, but it can augment us [in some domains] and do a much better job. But humans will still be super critical by 2060.*[214]

But better job performance aside, are AI and the Internet, social media in particular, making us better people? How is this information revolution influencing how we socially relate to one another—our sense of independent choice and personal initiative—our privacy of thought and actions?

Both for better and worse, these powerful social impacts will only become ever more profoundly pervasive.

The information revolution already enables users to create and exchange data with others from one end of the world to another in seconds; to make and share online presentations including videos, graphics, sound and text content; and yes, also to escape reality in virtual "game worlds."

The Weaponization of AI and the Internet

Social media connections through the Internet have forever changed our perceptions and realities of life and work opportunities and countless aspects of our daily living routines. The platform has altered the ways we interact with loved ones, friends, employers and clients; and has opened up new ways to identify and actively participate with groups and individuals who share special interests and problems.

E-Commerce has dramatically transformed the ways we acquire and provide goods and services. We can now book airline tickets and hotel reservations online; purchase an antique car part on eBay or an out-of-print book on Amazon; and even purchase fresh food with no need to travel to the grocery store. We don't even have to stand in bank lines anymore.

Since online shopping is removing the middleman, we can now purchase many of those products at much cheaper prices. Geographic distance is no longer a limit. The Internet has brought the power of online shopping and auctioning to people all over the world.

The Internet has freed us from geographic fetters and has connected us together in topic-based communities as a networked, globalized society connected by new technologies. It now provides much of our news and pundit views. It connects us with real-time updates about happenings around the world, including real-time sports and weather information.

We also have new means to broadly communicate our own views and creativity through blogs and books published through e-publishers. We can read them online or on Kindle. We advertise and transact our goods and services across oceans and deserts.

We now have just-in-time information about almost anything from anywhere. Print newspapers and magazines with dated information are being rapidly replaced by "news-breaking" electronic versions. Paperless record-keeping and publishing have replaced telephone books and cook books. Although not nearly as reliable, *Wikipedia* has replaced expensive and space-consuming sets of the *Encyclopedia Britanica*, which went out of print in 2011.

As blog writer Taryn Dentzel noted in an Openmind.com article, "How the Internet Has Changed Everyday Life:"

> *The future of social communications will be shaped by an 'always-online' culture. Always online is already here and will set the trend going forward. Total connectivity, the Internet, you can take with you wherever you go, is growing unstoppably. There is no turning back from global digitization.*[215]

Dentzel adds:

> *The Internet has turned our existence upside down. It has revolutionized communications, to the extent that it is now our preferred medium for everyday communication. In almost everything we do, we use Internet. Ordering a pizza, buying a television, sharing a moment with a friend, sending a picture over instant messaging. Before the Internet, if you wanted to keep up with the news, you had to walk down to the newsstand when it opened in the morning and buy a local edition reporting what had happened the previous day. But today a click or two is enough to read your local paper and any news source from anywhere in the world, updated to the minute.*

The Internet has removed previous communication barriers. Online, the conventional constraints of space and time disappear and there is a dizzyingly wide range of communicative possibilities where we can share private gossip and jokes, participate in and watch online conferences, and join special groups to keep abreast of their specific interests.

But these many advantages come with some catches...some

big ones.

As media philosopher Marshall McLuhan famously pointed out in the 1960s, media platforms are not just passive channels of information. His influential book, *Understanding Media,* emphasized ways that their effects actively permeate all aspects of society and culture.

McLuhan couldn't possibly have foreseen the dramatic and expansive technological influences that artificial intelligence, the Internet, social media and mobile smartphones would come to have on society. Nor could he have imagined the monopolistic power and influence that social media companies would come to wield over personal communications.

Social media tech behemoths have amassed astonishing economic lobbying swag and far-left-leaning ideological sway with rapidly expanding influences.

In 2018, four of the world's ten largest market cap corporations were Silicon Valley companies: Amazon ($860 billion), Microsoft ($833 billion), Alphabet-Google ($765 billion) and Facebook ($445 billion). Two of the remaining ten largest are Chinese information tech companies: Tencent ($496 billion) and Alibaba ($370 billion).

Big Tech company status as corporate—rather than government—entities currently entitles them to unaccountably determine what we are allowed to see, what we are not allowed to see and from whom, entirely at their own discretion.

There is no ambiguity regarding Silicon Valley's prevailing ideological bias.

Facebook, which together with Google controls 60 percent of all digital ad revenues, has blatantly blocked publishers from posting factual and opinion content that deviates from corporate ideology. Included are materials which are critical of socialist ideals, such as a paid video ad urging Millennials to embrace principles of individual liberty, personal responsibility and free enterprise and to reject radical collectivism of Karl Marx.

Exemptions from standard laws and regulations applied to

media publishers has assumed that social media companies would operate as impartial, open channels of communications—not curators of acceptable opinions. All-too-often, the absence of requisite neutrality leading to censorship and shadow banning calls the merit of such preferential exemptions into question.

A perhaps equally troubling alternative would contemplate putting political government bureaucrats in charge of determining regulatory boundaries regarding what constitutes prohibited so-called "hate speech" and the disseminations of "false information" advertisements. When people begin suggesting that certain communications and expressions be regulated, they are typically referring to those "other people's" communications and expressions.

Either way, those holding power—whether government or corporations—will control the flow of information and ideas. Hence, we all—ideologically left, right and center—face a common dilemma.

One strategy would grant more government regulatory intrusion in private markets; the other will continue to allow ever more powerful social media companies to silence whomever they don't agree with.

Those wonderful Internet social media platforms which enables us to locate, connect and interact with one another accordingly also pose real challenges which threaten our privacy and security.

Although we may expect that security measures have been put in place to keep such information confidential, world-wide criminal networks and individual hackers work persistently, sometimes successfully, to defeat even very advanced safeguards. Hence, an already vast number of victims continues to grow.

Computer hackers are literally stealing human identities. Whereas criminals have long-used discarded credit card receipts, bank statements, tax notices and other bills (often found in trash) to access personal information, today's electronic playing field has prompted cunning new theft methods.

Just as our online activities, including emails, information searches and website visits are constantly being monitored and stored, uninvited eavesdropping voice assistants can do the same. Whether spoken or typed, the messages leave behind a steady trail of recorded snippets which reveal special interests, habits and preferences that target subscribers for related advertising promotions and other purposes.

The wired-together Internet of Things now connects us through virtually every electronic device we own or use to vast networks of privacy-snooping and snitching data compilers and malevolent hackers. The range of such device vulnerabilities is vast and forever expanding. A small list of examples includes smart meters, thermostats, refrigerators, home security monitors, TVs, smart phones, web-connected cameras, and wearable fitness trackers and healthcare devices.[216]

Aggressively marketed "smart city" proposals promise to make our lives more efficient and safer through ubiquitous Internet-connected and centrally monitored personal, household, municipal and regional systems which will be capable of constantly tracking our locations, our activities, and our relationships with others.

Smart city messaging campaigns promote interconnected smart electrical meters, smart buildings, smart transportation services and smart citizen surveillance systems within smart grids. The idea is premised upon applying information and communication technologies (ICT) which collect and manage data on everything from air quality—to noise levels—to individual and group movements through an extensive network of sensors and surveillance cameras.

Smart city buyers beware! Such rhetoric energetically promulgated by big technology, engineering and consulting companies is predicated on the embedding of computerized sensors into the urban fabric so that bike racks and lamp posts, CCTV and traffic lights, remote-control air conditioning systems and home appliances all become interconnected into the wireless broadband Internet of Things.

The marketing campaigns are working. Global populations, Americans included, are trading away more and more of their personal privacy for promises of increased convenience and security.

Spy cameras are already sprouting up on lampposts and rooftops everywhere, facial recognition systems can track each of our individual movements and ICT and IoC networks are wiring private home appliances within municipal energy monitoring and eventual control networks overseen by George Orwell's Big Brother.

Smart city templates are guiding major international urban developments, ranging from Songdo, South Korea; to Dholera, India; to Rio de Janeiro, Brazil; to Cairo, Egypt; to Moscow, Russia; and of course, including expansively draconian population monitoring and social credit "merit assessment" networks throughout China.

Chinese officials are known to be actively marketing their advanced facial recognition and other technologies to numerous other countries including Russia, Egypt, Turkey and throughout Latin America. Ecuadorian law enforcement officials, for example, have purchased a network of Chinese security cameras with facial recognition software.[217]

The global client list of one such Chinese surveillance firm Tiandy, a CCTV camera manufacturer and "smart security solution provider," includes more than 60 countries.

These technologies offer great potential for repressive use against U.S. security interests. ZTE Corp., China's second largest telecommunications equipment maker, is known to have been helping the Iranian regime track dissidents since at least 2010.

Venezuelan strongman Nicolás Maduro's "homeland card" is used as a political control mechanism to control access to food and other social services and is modeled after China's social credit system.

President Trump signed an executive order in May 2019 to let the United States ban telecommunications gear from "foreign adversaries." Along with the executive order, the Commerce Department added China's Huawei Technologies Co. to a list of entities in activities that are contrary to U.S. interests. That restriction could restrict sales or transfers of American technology to Huawei by requiring a government license—a potential blow to the company, which relies on some U.S. tech companies for chips.

U.S. national security officials say that Chinese companies, including Huawei and ZTE Corp., pose a threat, since under China's Communist Party rule, they are obliged to abide by Beijing's orders.[218]

Whereas Huawei denied claims of suspected information piracy risks associated with their equipment and business, Timothy Heath, Senior International Defense Research Analyst at the Rand Corporation, believes differently. He reported:

> Huawei continues to receive contracts from the Chinese military to develop communications technologies. As of January, 2018, Huawei remained active in the 863 funding program [a program that utilizes private companies to develop technologies with commercial and military applications].[219]

Most concerning, big American tech companies are working with China to establish those widespread public monitoring and social media censorship systems.[220]

In October 2018, Vice President Mike Pence specifically called upon Google to "immediately end development of the Dragonfly app that will strengthen Communist Party censorship and compromise the privacy of Chinese customers."

Google has been far less cooperative with our own national interests. The company walked away from a Pentagon request to develop algorithms that will speed up the extraction of meaningful information from hours of mostly useless drone footage. Google also turned down a chance to participate in a ten-year project to build-out the military's cloud infrastructure.

Microsoft, Apple and Amazon have engineered special arrangements to comply with a new Chinese law mandating that all companies working in the country must store their proprietary data and source codes there.

We are witnessing a worldwide impact not only of AI and the internet, but also of the expanding powers of the overlords who control them in all social spheres: ethical, economic and political. As a result, two opposing attitudes have emerged: one that these influences will beneficially augment future lives and societies; the other that it will diminish them.

Most likely prospects hold that both predictions will be true.

There is virtually no likelihood that this revolutionary march of enrichment and encroachment upon all human domains will lose momentum. Rather, that momentum will only accelerate.

As Professor Justin Zobel, head of the Department of Computing & information Systems at the University of Melbourne, Australia, noted in his May 31, 2016 blog:

> *It is a truism that computing continues to change our world. It shapes how objects are designed, what information we receive, how and where we work, and who we meet and do business with. And computing changes our understanding of the world around us and the Universe beyond.*[221]

Zobel directs our awareness to a broad reality that this information revolution is advancing on separate, diverse tracks:

> *Each wave of new computational technology has tended to lead to new kinds of systems, new ways of*

creating tools, new forms of data, and so on, which have often overturned their predecessors. What has seemed to be evolution is, in some ways, a series of revolutions.

Adding to impacts of a mind-dumbing pace of AI computing advancements, the Internet-enabled social media has dramatically revolutionized communication in countless beneficial ways. Some of those Internet connected capabilities have a very dark and dangerous side as well as uninvited data miners and cyber criminals exploit our trust and complacency.

Those same AI and Internet technologies that support our private communications to one another also extend our security vulnerability to the interconnected electronic devices we install in our homes and personal workplaces to make our lives more convenient, efficient and satisfying. This includes smart thermostats that manage our heating needs, refrigerators that keep track of our food inventories, surveillance systems and displays showing today's weather or our latest emails or news as we shower.

Some 29 million American residences contained connected, smart-home devices in 2017...a number which has been growing at a rate of 31 percent each year. This growth trend will likely accelerate as emerging AI technologies including 5G make it easier and easier to automate repetitive aspects of our daily lives—as devices get even better at communicating with each other.

And yes, expect that those connected devices will be snitching lots of very personal information about you to some of the last people and organizations world-wide that you would want to have as confidants.

Lacking the apocalyptic drama of Hollywood blockbusters, some inherent complacency perils might be likened by to my previously mentioned "boiling frog" analogy. Like a hapless frog placed comfortably in an open container of tepid water which is then brought slowly to a boil, it will not perceive danger until it is too late to jump out and is cooked to death.

About the Author

LARRY BELL IS an Endowed Professor of Space Architecture at the University of Houston who founded the Sasakawa International Center for Space Architecture and its graduate program in Space architecture. Professor Bell has authored more than 600 editorial articles on a wide variety of topics for Forbes and Newsmax magazines, along with seven books.

This book extends and expands the theme and contents of a previous one also published this year titled *Reinventing Ourselves: How Technology is Rapidly and Radically Transforming Humanity*. Larry's other recent books include: *Thinking Whole: Rejecting Half-Witted Left and Right Brain Limitations*; *Scared Witless: Prophets and Profits of Climate Doom*; *Climate of Corruption: Politics and Power Behind the Global Warming Hoax*; *Reflections on Oceans and Puddles: One Hundred Reasons to be Enthusiastic, Grateful and Hopeful*; and *Cosmic Musings: Contemplating Life Beyond Self.*

As a tech entrepreneur, Larry co-founded an aerospace company with NASA's Chief Engineer and two other partners which grew through mergers and acquisitions to employ more than 8,000 professionals, went public on the New York Stock Exchange, and was purchased by General Dynamics. He holds two of the highest professional honors awarded by the Russian space program for his contributions to international space development, and his name was placed in large letters on the Russian rocket that launched the first crew to the International

Space Station.

Footnotes

[1] "Where machines could replace humans- and where they can't (yet)," Michael Chui, James Manyika, and Mehdi Miremadi, McKinsey Quarterly, July 2016.

[2] "The history of computing is both evolution and revolution," Justin Zobel, The Conversation.com, May 31, 2016.

[3] "Post-quantum cryptology—dealing with the fallout of physics success," Daniel J. Bernstein and Tanja Lange, National Science Foundation/European Commission, April 9, 2017.

[4] "Ken Olsen: Did Digital founder Ken Olsen say there was 'no reason for any individual to have a computer in his home"?, Snopes.com, https://www.snopes.com/fact-check/ken-olsen/.

[5] "Why GANs give artificial intelligence wonderful (and scary) capabilities," Gabriel Sidhom, August 23, 2017, Orangesv.com.

[6] Ibid.

[7] "The Machines That Will Read Your Mind," Jerry Kaplan, April 6-7, 2019, Wall Street Journal Review.

[8] Ibid.

[9] Ibid.

[10] "The truth about smart cities: 'In the end, they will destroy democracy,'" Steven Poole, December 17, 2014, The Guardian.

[11] "Stop Saying 'Smart Cities,'" Bruce Sterling, February 12, 2018, The Atlantic.com, Technology.

[12] "The smart entrepreneurial city: Dholera and 100 other utopias in India," S. Marvin, A. Luque-Ayala, and C McFarlane (Eds.), 2015, Smart urbanism: Utopian vision or false dawn?, Rutledge.

[13] "The truth about smart cities: 'In the end, they will destroy democracy,'" Steven Poole, December 17, 2014, The Guardian.

[14] Ibid.

[15] "Smart Cities and the Idea of Smartness in Urban Development—a Critical Review," Milan Husar, Vladimir Oudrejieka and Sila Ceren Varis, 2017, IOP Conference Series; Materials Science and Engineering, 245.

[16] " Ibid.

[17] "The Autocrat's New Tool Kit," Richard Fountaine and Kara Frederick, March 15, 2019, Wall Street Journal.

[18] "From Falun Gong to Xinjiang: China's Repression Maestro", Chun Han Wong, April 4, 2019, Wall Street Journal.

[19] Ibid.

[20] Ibid.

[21] "China selling high-tech tyranny to Latin America, stoking US concern," Joel Gehrke, April 10. 2016, The Washington Examiner.

[22] "The Autocrat's New Tool Kit," Richard Fontaine and Kara Frederick, March 16-17, Wall Street Journal Review Section.

[23] "The Pros and Cons of Facial Recognition," Ted Rall, May 16, 2019, The Wall Street Journal.

[24] "The Autocrat's New Tool Kit," Richard Fontaine and Kara Frederick, March 16-17, 2019, Wall Street Journal Review Section.

[25] Ibid.

[26] Ibid.

[27] Ibid.

[28] Ibid.

[29] Ibid.

[30] Ibid.

[31] "Gifts That Snoop? The Internet of Things Is Wrapped in Privacy Concerns," Bree Fowler, December 13, 2017, Consumer Reports.

[32] "FTC WARNS OF SECURITY AND PRIVACY RISKS IN IOT DEVICES," Pindrop.com.

[33] "The Autocrat's New Tool Kit," Richard Fontaine and Kara Frederick, March 16-17, Wall Street Journal Review Section.

[34] "FTC WARNS OF SECURITY AND PRIVACY RISKS IN IOT DEVICES," Pindrop.com.

[35] "The Autocrat's New Tool Kit," Richard Fontaine and Kara Frederick, March 16-17, 2019, Wall Street Journal Review Section.

[36] "Facebook artificial intelligence spots suicidal users," Leo Kelion, March 1, 2017, BBC News.

[37] "Deep Learning 'Godfather' Bengio Worries About China's Use of AI," Jeremy Kahn, February 2, 2019, Bloomberg.

[38] "The Autocrat's New Tool Kit," Richard Fontaine and Kara Frederick, March 16-17, 2019, Wall Street Journal Review Section.

[39] "AI as Servants or Spies," John Edwards, Newsmax, October 2017.

[40] "Rise of the Robots," Stephen Moore, Newsmax, October 2017.

[41] "AI as Servants or Spies?" John Edwards, Newsmax, October 2017.

[42] "Your phone is like a spy in your pocket." January 24, 2018, Applone Infotech, http://apploneinfotech.com/your-phone-is-like-a-spy-in-your-

pocket/#about-us.

[43] "AI as Servants or Spies," John Edwards, Newsmax, October 2017.

[44] "Yahoo, Bucking Industry, Scans Emails for Data to Sell," Douglas MacMillan, Sarah Krouse and Keach Hagey, August 8, 2018, Wall Street Journal.

[45] Ibid.

[46] "Your Phone Is Listening and it's Not Paranoia," Sam Nichols, June 4, 2018, Vice.com.

[47] Ibid.

[48] "When a smart home becomes a trap," Robby Berman, July 1, 2018, New York Times.

[49] Internet of Business.com "Security: The IOT is destroying legal concept of privacy warns in-depth report," Chris Middleton, June 15, 2018, referencing a 150-page document, "Clearly Opaque: Privacy Risks of the IoT," the Internet of Things Forum, 2018, https://www.iotprivacyforum.org/clearlyopaque/.

[50] Internet of Business.com "Security: The IOT is destroying legal concept of privacy warns in-depth report," Chris Middleton, June 15, 2018.

[51] Ibid.

[52] Wall Street Journal: "Artificial Intelligence," April 2, 2019: "Will AI Destroy More Jobs Than It Creates Over the Next Decade?," Article, "What AI Can Tell from Listening to You," John McCormick, Deputy director of WSJ Pro Artificial Intelligence in New York.

[53] Internet of Business.com "Security: The IOT is destroying legal concept of privacy warns in-depth report", Chris Middleton, June 15, 2018, referencing a 150-page document, "Clearly Opaque: Privacy Risks of the IoT," the Internet of Things Forum, 2018, https://www.iotprivacyforum.org/clearlyopaque/.

[54] Wall Street Journal: "Artificial Intelligence," April 2, 2019: "Will AI Destroy More Jobs Than It Creates Over the Next Decade?," Article, "What AI Can Tell from Listening to You," John McCormick, Deputy Director of WSJ Pro Artificial Intelligence in New York.

[55] Internet of Business.com "Security: The IOT is destroying legal concept of privacy warns in-depth report", Chris Middleton, June 15, 2018, referencing a 150-page document, "Clearly Opaque: Privacy Risks of the IoT", the Internet of Things Forum, 2018, https://www.iotprivacyforum.org/clearlyopaque/.

[56] "Confirmed: Facebook's Recent Algorithm Change Is Crushing Conservative Sites, Boosting Liberals," George Upper and Shaun Hair,

October 25, 2018, The Western Journal.com.

[57] "When Social media platforms Block Conservatives," John Stossel, October 17, 2018, Reason.

[58] "Trump Says Google, Facebook, Amazon May BE 'Antitrust Situation,'" John Micklethwait, Margaret Talev and Jennifer Jacobs, August 30, 2028, Bloomberg.

[59] "Social Media and Censorship," Francis Fukuyama, August 8, 2018, The American Interest.

[60] "Yahoo, Bucking Industry, Scans Emails for Data to Sell," Douglas MacMillan, Sarah Krouse and Keach Hagey, August 8, 2018, Wall Street Journal.

[61] "How the Internet Has changed Everyday Life", Zaryn Dentzel, Openmind.com.

[62] "Couples, the Internet, and Social Media, How American couples use digital technology to manage life, logistics, and emotional intimacy within their relationships," Amanda Lenhart and Maeve Duggan, February 11, 2014, Pew Research Center, Internet & Technology http://www.pewinternet.org/2014/02/11/couples-the-internet-and-social-media/.

[63] "How is the Internet changing the way we behave?," Mary Aiken, March 27, 2017, Science Focus.com.

[64] "How is the Internet changing the way we behave?, Mary Aiken, March 27, 2017, Science Focus.com.

[65] "Cyberbullying websites should be boycotted, says Cameron; prime Minister calls for website operators to 'step up to the plate,' following death of 14-yeat-old Hannah Smith," Alexandra Topping, Ellen Coyne and agencies, August 8, 2013, The Guardian.

[66] "Increase in Youth Suicide Prompts States to Act," Michael Ollove, September 28, 2016, PEW Health.

[67] "The Relationship Between Bullying and Suicide: What We Know and What it Means for Schools," Centers for Disease Control.

[68] "Have Smartphones Destroyed a Generation," Jean Twenge, September 2017, The Atlantic.

[69] "The Effect OF Technology On Relationships," Alex Lickerman, M.D., June 8, 2010, Psychology today.com, https://www.psychologytoday.com/us/blog/happiness-in-world/201006/the-effect-technology-relationships.

[70] "What Is the Internet Doing to Relationships?" John B. Horrigan, Barry Wellman and Jerry Boase, Pew Research Center, Internet and Technology,

January 25, 2006 http://www.pewinternet.org/2006/01/25/what-is-the-internet-doing-to-relationships/.

[71] "Where Do Humans Outperform AI?", Kevin McCaney, April 4, 2016, Bloomberg Government CIO Media.

[72] "20 Industries Threatened by Tech Disruption," Adam Hayes, Investopedia, Feb. 6, 2015.

[73] "Lectures on Economic Growth," Robert Lucas, 2002, Cambridge: Harvard University Press.

[74] "Technological Transformations and Long Waves," Robert Ayres, 1989, PDF.

[75] "Sapiens: A Brief History of Humankind," Yuval Noah Harari, New York, London, Toronto, Sydney, New Delhi, Auckland: HarperCollins/Harper Perennial, 2015.

[76] "The history of computing is both evolution and revolution," Justin Zobel, The Conversation.com, May 31, 2016.

[77] https://alleninstitute.org/what-we-do/brain-science/about/team/staff-profiles/christof-koch/.

[78] "Inside the New Industrial Revolution," Christopher Mims, November 18, 2018, The Wall Street Journal, Technology.

[79] "Inside the New Industrial Revolution," Christopher Mims, November 18, 2018, The Wall Street Journal, Technology.

[80] "Jobs lost, jobs gained: What the future of work will mean for jobs, skills and wages," McKinsey & Company, James Manyika, Susan Lund, Michael Chui, Jacques Bughin, Jonathan Woetzel, Paul Batra, Ryan Ko, and Saurabh Sanghvi, November 2017.

[81] "Where machines could replace humans—and where they can't (yet)," Michael Chui and James Manyika, 2016, McKinsey Quarterly.

[82] "Artificial Intelligence: Will AI Destroy More Jobs Than It Creates Over the Next Decade?: What AI Will Do to Corporate Hierarchies," Thomas W. Malone, April 2, 2019, Wall Street Journal.

[83] "Where machines could replace humans—and where they can't (yet)," Michal Chui, James Manyika, and Mehdi Miremadi, McKinsey Quarterly, McKinsey & Company, July 20, 2016.

[84] "Jobs lost, jobs gained: What the future of work will mean for jobs, skills and wages," McKinsey & Company, James Manyika, Susan Lund, Michael Chui, Jacques Bughin, Jonathan Woetzel, Paul Batra, Ryan Ko, and Saurabh Sanghvi, November 2017.

[85] "Where machines could replace humans—and where they can't (yet)," Michal Chui, James Manyika, and Mehdi Miremadi, McKinsey Quarterly,

McKinsey & Company, July 20, 2016.

[86] "Artificial Intelligence: Will AI Destroy More Jobs Than It Creates Over the Next Decade?" April 2, 2019: Wall Street Journal.

[87] "Every study we could find on what automation will do to jobs, in one chart," Erin Winick, MIT Technology Review.com, January 25, 2018.

[88] "20 Industries Threatened by Tech Disruption," Adam Hayes, Investopedia, Feb. 6, 2015.

[89] Ibid.

[90] "11 Industries Being Disrupted By AI," David Roe, CMS Wire.com, April 27, 2018.

[91] "5 Fast-growing Technology Trends for 2017," Cynthia Harvey, Cloud Infrastructure, McAfee, Jan. 11, 2017.

[92] "Jobs lost, jobs gained: What the future of work will mean for jobs, skills and wages," McKinsey & Company, James Manyika, Susan Lund, Michael Chui, Jacques Bughin, Jonathan Woetzel, Paul Batra, Ryan Ko, and Saurabh Sanghvi, November 2017.

[93] "Why Robots Will Not Take Over Human Jobs," Andrew Arnold, March 27, 2018, Forbes.com.

[94] "How AI Is Transforming The Future Of Healthcare," Gunjan Bhardwaj, Forbes.com, Jan. 30, 2018.

[95] "Artificial Intelligence in Healthcare: Separating Reality From Hype," Robert Pearl, Forbes.com, March 13, 2018.

[96] "Tomorrow's Lawyers: An Introduction to Your Future," Richard Susskind, Oxford University Press, 1999, ISBN 978019968069.

[97] "Legal Technology: Artificial Intelligence and the Future of Law Practice," Mark McKamey, Appeal Law Journal—Vol. 22, Citation (2017) Appeal 45.

[98] "Use of AI in Banking is Set to Explode," Jim Marcus, January 17, 2017, The Financial Brand.

[99] "Industrial robots will replace manufacturing jobs—and that's a good thing," Matthew Randall, TechCrunch.com, October 9, 2016.

[100] "The 3-D Printing Revolution," Richard D'Aveni, Harvard Business Review, May 2015 Issue.

[101] "The Human Promise of the AI Revolution," Kai-Fu Lee, September 15-16, 2018, Wall Street Journal.

[102] "Why Free Money for Everyone is Silicon Valley's Next Big Idea," Clay Dillow and Brooks Rainwater, June 29, 2017, Fortune.

[103] Ibid.

[104] "Universal Basic income: A Universally Bad Idea," Marco Annunziata, July 27, 2018, Forbes.

[105] "AI Is Here to Stay. What That Means Is Still Developing," Sara Castellanos, October 27-28, 2018, Wall Street Journal Technology.

[106] "Conservatives and politics of Work," Jason Willick, November 24-24, Wall Street Journal.

[107] "Out of the Office: More People Are Working Remotely, Survey Finds Out of the Office: More People Are Working Remotely, Survey Finds," Niraj Chokshi, February 15, 2017, the NewYorkTimes.com.

[108] "Why Remote Work Thrives in Some Companies and Fails in Others," Sean Graber, March 20, 2015, Harvard Business Review.

[109] "How Remote Work Is Changing And What It Means For Your Future," William Arruda, February 16, 2017, Forbes.com.

[110] "The Future of Home Business Technology," Tiffany S. Williams, December 11, 2017, Forbes.com.

[111] "Benefits of Telecommuting For The Future of Work," Andrea Loubier, July 20, 2017, Forbes.com.

[112] "New poll of rural Americans shows deep cultural divide with urban centers," Jose A. Delreal and Scott Clement, June 17, 2017, The Washington Post.

[113] "Government Can't Rescue the Poor," Phil Gramm and John E. Early, October 11, Wall Street Journal.

[114] "The Differences Between City, Suburban, and Rural Living," February 2, 2018, Property Management, Inc., https://www.rentmi.com.

[115] Ibid.

[116] "How Driverless Cars Will Change the Feel of Cities," Ian Bogoost, November 15, 2017, The Atlantic.com.

[117] "Self-driving cars will set off an economic and cultural earthquake," Eric Risberg, May 11, 2018, The Global Mail.com.

[118] "How Driverless Cars Will Change the Feel of Cities", Ian Bogoost, November 15, 2017, The Atlantic.com.

[119] "We let technology into our lives. And now it's starting to control us," Rachel Holmes, November 28, 2016, The Guardian.com.

[120] Ibid.

[121] "The truth about smart cities: 'In the end, they will destroy democracy,'" Steven Poole, December 17, 2014, The Guardian.

[122] "Who Can You Trust? How Technology Brought Us Together and Why It Might Drive Us Apart," Rachel Botsman, (2017) Penguin Books.

[123] "A Global Tech Backlash," Christopher Mims, October 27-28, 2018, Wall Street Journal, Technology.

[124] "Ex-Google engineer who worked on China search engine calls out

'wrong,'" Daniel Howley, September 19, 2018, Yahoo Finance.

[125] "A Global Tech Backlash," Christopher Mims, October 27-28, 2018, Wall Street Journal, Technology.

[126] Ibid.

[127] Ibid.

[128] "Sri Lanka's social media shutdown illustrates global discontent with Silicon Valley," Tony Romm, Elizabeth Dwoskin and Craig Timberg, April 22, 2019 The Washington Post.

[129] Ibid.

[130] Ibid.

[131] Ibid.

[132] "Fear Mark Zuckerberg's Illiberal Impulses," Kevin D. Williamson, April 25, 2019, Wall Street Journal.

[133] Ibid.

[134] Ibid.

[135] "Regulate social media now. The future is at stake," Anne Applebaum, February 1, 2019, The Washington Post.

[136] Ibid.

[137] Ibid.

[138] Ibid.

[139] "Mueller Report: Special Counsel Didn't Examine DNC Servers—Based on FBI Investigation that Didn't Examine DNC Servers," Aaron Klein, May 1, 2019, Breitbart.

[140] Ibid.

[141] Ibid.

[142] Ibid.

[143] Ibid.

[144] "What Is the Dark Web—Who Uses It, Dangers & Precautions to Take," Michael Lewis, May 2019, Moneycrashers.

[145] "Deeplight: Shining the Light On the Dark Web," An Intelliagg Report, 2016.

[146] "What Is the Dark Web—Who Uses It, Dangers & Precautions to Take," Michael Lewis, May 2019, Moneycrashers.

[147] "The most Dangerous Hackers Today," Joseph Regan, July 24, 2018, AVG.com.

[148] Ibid.

[149] "It's not just Russia. China, north Korea, and Iran could interfere in 2018 elections too," Alex Ward, August 20, 2018, Vox.

[150] "The most Dangerous Hackers Today," Joseph Regan, July 24, 2018,

AVG.com.

[151] "New Chinese Hacker Group Linked to 'One Belt, One Road' Initiative," Frank Fang, March 7-13, The Epoch Times.

[152] "The most Dangerous Hackers Today," Joseph Regan, July 24, 2018, AVG.com.

[153] Ibid.

[154] "North Korea hackers are targeting 'critical' U.S. infrastructure, a cybersecurity firm says," Donie O'Sullivan and Joshua Berlinger, March 5, 2019, CNN.

[155] "The most Dangerous Hackers Today," Joseph Regan, July 24, 2018, AVG.com.

[156] "Are we underestimating Iran's cyber capabilities?," Annie Fixler, March 11, 2919, The Hill.

[157] "2 Iranian men indicted for city of Atlanta ransomware attack," November 28, 2018, Fox 5 Atlanta.

[158] Ibid.

[159] "Confidential Report: Atlanta's cyber attack could cost taxpayers $17 million," Stephen Deere, August 1, 2018, The Atlanta Journal-Constitution.

[160] Ibid.

[161] Ibid.

[162] "Pence Cautions Google on China," Michael C. Bender and Dustin Volz, October 5, 2018. Wall Street Journal.

[163] "Ex-Google engineer who worked on China search engine calls out 'wrong,'" Daniel Howley, September 19, 2018, Yahoo Finance.

[164] "The ethics of Artificial Intelligence," Justin Lee, June 26, 2018, GrowthBot.org.

[165] "Beijing Expands Its Cybersecurity Regulations," Shan Li, October 6-7, 2018, Wall Street Journal.

[166] "Ibid.

[167] "The Big Hack: How China Used a Tiny Chip to Infiltrate U.S. Companies," October 4, 2018, Bloomberg Businessweek.

[168] Ibid.

[169] "Exclusive: FBI probes FDIC hack linked to China's military—sources," Dustin Volz and jason Lang, December 23, 2016, Reuters World News.

[170] "The Big Hack: How China Used a Tiny Chip to Infiltrate U.S. Companies," October 4, 2018, Bloomberg Businessweek.

[171] "Code: And Other Laws of Cyberspace, Version 2.0/Edition 2," Lawrence Lessig, December 28, 2006, Basic Books.

[172] "The imaginary real world of cybercities," M.C. Boyer, 1992, Assemblage.

[173] "A model Korean ubiquitous eco-city? The politics of making Songdo," S.T. Shwayri, 2013, Journal of Urban Technology.

[174] "They Are Watching You," Robert Draper, February 2018, National Geographic.

[175] Ibid

[176] Ibid

[177] Ibid.

[178] Ibid

[179] Ibid

[180] "Welcome to the Quiet Skies," Jana Winter, July 28, 2018, the Boston Globe.

[181] Ibid.

[182] "We let technology into our lives. And now it's starting to control us," Rachel Holmes, November 28, 2016, The Guardian.com.

[183] "The Jeep hack was only the beginning of smart car breaches," Cadie Thompson, July 22, 2015, Business Insider.com.

[184] "Hackers Might be Able to Take Control of your Smart Car," Michael Aechambault, March 9, 2018, PSafe.com.

[185] "How Driverless Cars Will Change the Feel of Cities," Ian Bogoost, November 15, 2017, The Atlantic.com.

[186] https://alleninstitute.org/what-we-do/brain-science/about/team/staff-profiles/christof-koch/.

[187] "The Human Promise of the AI Revolution," Kai-Fu Lee, September 15-16, 2018, Wall Street Journal.

[188] Ibid.

[189] "Trading Places," Liz Hoffman and Telis Demos, August 18, 2018, Wall Street Journal.

[190] Ibid.

[191] "Commentary: The biggest risk to the market? The market itself," Jamie McGeever, February 6, 2018, UK, Reuters.com.

[192] "The stock market is controlled by algorithms that are fighting with each other," Annalee Newitz, May 11, 2011, i09.gizmodo.com.

[193] "Models Will Run the World," Steven A. Cohen and Matthew W. Granade, Wall Street Journal, August 20, 2018.

[194] "Artificial intelligence—can we keep it in the box?," Huw Price and Jean Tallinn, The Conversation.com.

[195] Ibid.

[196] "Stephen Hawking: Artificial Intelligence Could Wipe Out Humanity When It Gets Too Clever As Humans Will be like Ants," Andrew Griffin,

October 8, 2015, Independent.co.uk.

[197] Ibid.

[198] Ibid

[199] Ibid

[200] "The Human Promise of the AI Revolution," Kai-Fu Lee, September 15-16, 2018, Wall Street Journal.

[201] "Technology isn't just changing society—it's changing what it means to be human: A conversation with historian of science Michael Bess," Sean Illing, February 23, 2018, Vox.com.

[202] Phaedrus, section 275d.

[203] "Technology isn't just changing society—it's changing what it means to be human: A conversation with historian of science Michael Bess," Sean Illing, February 23, 2018, Vox.com.

[204] Ibid.

[205] Ibid.

[206] Information Technology and Moral Values," Stanford Encyclopedia of Philosophy, June 12, 2012.

[207] Ibid.

[208] "On the Intrinsic Value of Information Objects and the Infosphere," L. Floridi, 2003, Ethics and Information Technology, 4(4): 287-304.

[209] "Artificial intelligence—can we keep it in the box?", Huw Price and Jean Tallinn, The Conversation.com.

[210] Ibid.

[211] Jobs lost, jobs gained: What the future of work will mean for jobs, skills and wages, McKinsey & Company, James Manyika, Susan Lund, Michael Chui, Jacques Bughin, Jonathan Woetzel, Paul Batra, Ryan Ko, and Saurabh Sanghvi, November 2017.

[212] "The Human Promise of the Revolution," Kai-Fu Lee, September 15-16, Wall Street Journal (DR. Lee is chairman and CEO of Sinovation Ventures and former president of Google China. This referenced essay is adapted from Dr. Lee's new book: "AI Superpowers: China, Silicon Valley and the New World Order," Houghton Mifflin Harcourt.

[213] Journalist Alisa Vakludes Whyte rhetorically asks in a June 25, 2017 Huffington Post article: "Will AI Best All Humans Tasks by 2060? Experts Say Not So Fast."

[214] "Will AI Best All Humans Tasks by 2060? Experts Say Not So Fast," Alisa Vakludes Whyte, Huffington Post, June 25, 2017.

[215] "How the Internet Has changed Everyday Life," Taryn Dentzel, Openmind.com.

[216] "Gifts That Snoop? The Internet of Things Is Wrapped in Privacy Concerns," Bree Fowler, December 13, 2017, Consumer Reports.

[217] "From Falun Gong to Xinjiang: China's Repression Maestro," Chun Han Wong, April 4, 2019, Wall Street Journal.

[218] "Telecom Ban Takes Aim at China," May 16, 2018, The Wall Street Journal.

[219] "Is Huawei a genuine Security Threat," September 12, 2018, Tech.co.

[220] "China selling high-tech tyranny to Latin America, stoking US concern," Joel Gehrke, April 10. 2016, The Washington Examiner.

[221] "The history of computing is both evolution and revolution," Justin Zobel, The Conversation.com, May 31, 2016.